CHRISTIAN RESPONSIBILITY

ROSEMARY HAUGHTON

CHRISTIAN
RESPONSIBILITY

SHEED AND WARD
LONDON AND NEW YORK

FIRST PUBLISHED 1964
SHEED AND WARD LTD
33 MAIDEN LANE
LONDON W.C.2
AND
SHEED AND WARD INC
64 UNIVERSITY PLACE
NEW YORK 3

NIHIL OBSTAT: JOANNES M. T. BARTON, S.T.D., L.S.S.

IMPRIMATUR ✠ GEORGIUS L. CRAVEN,
EPŪS SEBASTOPOLIS, VIC. GEN.

WESTMONASTERII, DIE 24a AUG. 1964

The *Nihil obstat* and *Imprimatur* are a declaration that a
book or pamphlet is considered to be free from doctrinal or
moral error. It is not implied that those who have granted
the *Nihil obstat* and *Imprimatur* agree with the contents,
opinions or statements expressed.

This book is set in 11 pt. Linotype Baskerville

Made and printed in Great Britain by
William Clowes and Sons, Limited, London and Beccles

CONTENTS

FOREWORD

THESE essays were all written out of a personal need to think out certain aspects of contemporary life in a Christian context. They all deal with subjects which concern ordinary people more or less closely, and can in many cases become agonizing moral problems. These subjects do not seem to feature in the "spiritual reading" recommended to Catholics, and so although I can claim no special authority or qualifications, these attempts to think out certain subjects as honestly as possible may perhaps stimulate others who feel a like need to spring-clean their ideas.

I wish to acknowledge my indebtedness to the editors of *The Life of the Spirit, The Aylesford Review, Search* and *Marriage,* in which some of these essays first appeared in article form.

R. H.

Christmas 1963

THINK FOR YOURSELF

O NE of the accusations most often levelled
at Catholics—and other Christians too,
but with less conviction—is that they
are not allowed to think for themselves. Sometimes all it means is that the accuser resents any
profoundly held belief because he is too lazy
to bother to work out his own. He exalts his
mental and physical sloth into a virtue and
calls it "broadmindedness". But it is often the
result of a sincere conviction that it is ultimately
nobler to continue searching and uncertain than
to accept the comfort and support of a fixed
system of belief. Vita Sackville-West, in her
book on the two Teresas, *The Eagle and the
Dove*, describes the Catholic Church as "excellently suited to those whose temperament con-
forms to herd-obedience rather than the query-
ing recalcitrance of individualism. No room is
provided for the refractory, but along the eternal
corridor an endless succession of cells nine foot
by nine for the docile. Acceptance is the key-
note, and how delicious the repose when once
acceptance has been accomplished! Only the
misfit, the rebel, lonely in a world with different
values, perhaps can estimate the consolation of

finding himself at last with a company whose aims are entirely similar to his own. No longer a plant blown this way and that by the gale, his precarious roots loosened as he roughly sways, a strong stake now holds him fast, implacable wire engages his tendrils and above his roots a mulch centuries old in richness keeps him fed and cool. And as for the cell, it may be true that restricted measurements metaphorically harder than concrete define him, but there is no true duress here: the window is open over a landscape of unimaginable beauty, a liberty of spirit unknown even to the lark—nay, the very ceiling is off, open unlimited to a visionary height of his own and personal Heaven."

I have chosen this passage, which reflects the attitude of many intellectuals to the Church, because it shows a real effort at generosity. The author is trying to understand what it is that can make the restrictions she describes worth while. She recognizes honestly the greatness of certain Christians, and wants to appreciate the motives that can make them accept what seem to her intolerable limitations on human liberty. Yet although she acknowledges the new dimension to which this apparently narrow intellectual life gives access she cannot help feeling that such acceptance is unworthy, basically a surrender of freedom for the sake of spiritual comfort and security. "Herd-obedience", "docile", "acceptance", "repose", "consolation"—all these words show that for all her gallant attempt to be fair, the author cannot repress a fundamental contempt for those who have sold their birthright of intellectual freedom for a mess of spiritual pottage.

This is a very irritating passage, and it is easy to dismiss it as simply the result of pride and prejudice. But the fact that Christians find this accusation so irritating is a sign that they feel themselves to be in a vulnerable position. How much truth is there in the accusation? Can we really reconcile freedom and authority? Do we too easily accept what we are told? How much of our faith do we really believe, and how much do we simply preserve as a closed formula, without examining it?

To accept the authority of the Church is a free act, and as such it involves no loss of freedom. This acceptance can bring a sense of satisfaction and comfort, akin to the satisfaction anyone feels who has discovered at last a truth for which he has long been searching. This comfort, this sense of security, is not the thing sought, but the proper and natural result of the satisfaction of a fundamental craving for truth. It is as natural and right as the sense of well-being that comes from a good meal after a long day's work. There is no surrender of freedom here, only the proper exercise of that freedom, leading to a proper satisfaction in the result.

But there is too much truth in the accusation that Christians very often use their certainty of the Church's custody of truth as an excuse for leaving that truth untested. The acceptance of her authority is regarded as the end of the process of truth-seeking. The Church holds God's truth, all we need do is assent. Sometimes this attitude is part of a simple piety that is busy practising Christianity and feels no need to question the content of its faith. Such acceptance is sufficient in a closed society that takes Christian values for granted even if it does not always practise them. Sometimes such uncritical assent is a deliberate choice. The believer honestly thinks that it is wrong for him to examine what God sees fit to reveal to him through his Church. Sometimes it is due to mere laziness, culpable or not.

And sometimes the content of belief is not examined because the believer is afraid, though he would not admit it, that his beliefs would not stand up to examination. He is afraid that if he turned on his faith too strong a light he would discover such flaws and holes in it that he would no longer feel secure inside it. This reluctance to examine too closely may even be explicitly justified: human reason is fallible, and we can honestly reach quite erroneous conclusions. It is better not to risk heresy; rather, let us play safe and leave the explanation of doctrine to properly qualified persons. Circumstances of history have at times made such an attitude understandable, even necessary. Whether it was ever a good one is more doubtful. That it is not a good one now is clear enough. The first duty of a human being is to be honest with himself. If his honest processes of thought lead him, because of intellectual limitations or unconscious motivations, to objectively erroneous conclusions, his duty to abide by these conclusions remains. Those who recognize his error have also the duty of assisting him, if possible, to think his way out of it. But the correction of the error must be his own free and honest act. This supreme right to freedom of conscience has long seemed obvious to most thoughtful people. It is astonishing, a matter for serious self-questioning in the Church, that so many Catholics should have required a recent pronouncement on freedom of conscience from high authority in the Church before they felt themselves free to assent to it. This hesitation in giving assent to such a fundamental condition of human dignity and freedom is itself a glaring example of that failure to examine the implications of the Christian faith which prompted this investigation. There is all the difference in the world between holding an honestly argued conclusion with the sensible reservation that one may for some reason have concluded wrongly, and refusing to conclude anything lest that conclusion turn out to be apparently contrary to the teaching of the Church. This refusal to think for ourselves because of fear of error is just what non-Christians hold against members of the Church. To the extent to which this accusation is justified we are not only giving scandal to those outside the Church but betraying our trust as members of Christ.

The General Council was called for the purpose of re-presenting the teaching of the Church in a manner which would be acceptable to people of the twentieth century. This does not mean watering down ancient doctrines until they are acceptable to weak stomachs. It means making an honest effort to find out what these fundamental doctrines really mean. This may involve to some extent "forgetting" the understanding of them which has been reached in past centuries. Perhaps it was a perfect one: or perhaps it was a true but incomplete one; perhaps it was expressed in words that now carry a different significance. Whatever the virtues or defects of past definitions, they have to be laid aside in order to try to re-present the truth in the best way that can be achieved now.

But any achievement of this kind by the bishops in council may well be partly nullified if the faithful simply wait with open mouths to swallow the new presentation of the Faith like seals waiting for fish. Devotion to the Holy See and to the *magisterium* of the Church does not mean we have to devour whole all pronouncements of the teaching Church. Real devotion to the Holy See should mean trying to do as individuals and as local groups what the Church as a whole is trying to do: rethink our own faith.

It is often forgotten or not fully appreciated that all expressions of religious truth must necessarily be metaphorical. Sometimes the metaphors are simple and their significance immediately clear, their message illuminating, as in the most familiar of all metaphorical expressions of Christian teaching, that of Father, Son and Breath in the Trinity. These are Christ's chosen symbols to express the nature of God in human terms, and though others have been used these must have a special value. But some symbolic expressions of Christian understanding of truth have been more complex, have dealt in words that have, from the layman's point of view, so learned and abstruse an appearance that their metaphorical nature has been obscured and they have come to be treated as if they were not metaphorical at all. This has been true of scholastic jargon (using the word in no pejorative sense but simply as meaning specialist words devised to facilitate and clarify a particular skill or discipline) which has acquired such an aura of sanctity that its concepts, symbolic as all philosophical concepts must be, are often treated as if they were absolute, irreducible truth rather than a tested and valuable but fallible tool for investigating the ultimately undiscoverable.

But whether the metaphors that seek to express truth are simple and telling or complex and subtle, they can be not only valueless but actually dangerous when they are accepted as substitutes for the thing they strive to express. This is why truth can become stale, a revelation of new life stiffen into a conventional code.

Then the truth behind the words must be sought all over again, if need be in new words with the help of new philosophical disciplines; not because the old ways were bad but because ways of thinking and feeling have changed and modern minds may feel as ill at ease in medieval thought forms as modern bodies would feel in medieval clothes. The cast of a provincial historical pageant, however colourful, does not seem likely to provide suitable recruits for twentieth-century world leadership. This fact has been obvious for some time to many distinguished Christians not in communion with Rome. But not only to them. The Second Vatican Council has given public expression to some of the ideas that have in fact been discussed among certain groups of Catholics for many years, though the fear of error, corporately expressed in the official organs of the Church but also to be found undermining the confidence of the individual, made it necessary for these discussions to be virtually secret. This shameful episode in the history of the Church is, we hope, over. An era of discovery and reassessment has begun, and although some "new" ideas (which usually turn out to have a respectable ancestry) may sometimes seem a little unnerving at first they do at least make smugness, that besetting sin of orthodoxy, virtually impossible.

But it is not enough to remain spectators while the theological Jacobs wrestle with the angel and extort a blessing for us. One cannot

get Christianity at second hand. Though the
flame must be passed from one to another the
experience must be a personal one, in the intellectual as well as in the spiritual field (though
to separate the two even verbally is probably to
beg one of the many questions we have to try
to answer). But the ordinary lay person cannot
possibly keep up with all the movements of
thought in the Church, nor would such intellectual gymnastics be in keeping with his role
in the life of the Church.

If the moment ever comes when the "faith
committed to the Apostles" has been unfolded
and understood in every possible way, every implication discovered and lived, that moment will
be the last of our world. It is impossible for even
the greatest of theologians to understand in its
fullness every aspect of his faith. To assent to
certain things without much examination because reliable authority tells you this is God's
revelation is not the kind of intellectual laziness
or cowardice we have to try to avoid. It only becomes sloth or cowardice if we accept these doctrines with the implicit intention of not
examining them. But these unexamined truths
remain, for the individual, dormant and not
active truths. It is not necessary or even possible
for all the doctrines of the Faith to be equally
active influences in every life, but it is necessary
that some be active, or the Christian life in that
individual remains much the same as life in the
unborn foetus. All the faculties are present but

none is in use. If this state of affairs continues after birth we know that the individual is a hopeless imbecile. Religious imbeciles may be free of all blame but they are not much use to the Church.

Which particular aspects of truth engage the interest and rouse the conscience of the individual is a very personal matter. Age, temperament, career, nationality, health, education—all these and many other factors can help decide it. And one discovery leads to another. Changing circumstances raise new problems and offer fresh challenges. The Christian life should show a ceaseless development of understanding.

This is not true for intellectuals only. It used to be a favourite gambit of popular moralists to point out that the simple peasant often has a truer insight into the real meaning of religion than the highly educated man. Those better acquainted with the simple peasant may be inclined to raise an eyebrow, but it is certainly true that it is not education as such but honesty and integrity of mind and spirit that lead to true understanding. On the other hand, a greater responsibility lies on the educated to make use of their intellectual equipment to understand the faith they profess. It is the articulate minority who help both to express and to evolve the general understanding of the Faith from one generation to another.

The interesting thing, however, is that, while general and deliberate study of the content of

Christian teaching is the necessary prerequisite, the real and personal understanding of any one aspect of truth will almost always be the result of a personal and particular need, problem, desire, ambition.

Among the motives that drive to a new examination of some teaching of the Church it is particularly useful to consider one in particular. This motive for a deepening of understanding is the effect of an attack from outside on some doctrine, hitherto accepted without examination, either in a newspaper or book, or in conversation. Such an attack can have two different effects on the believer. He can set about refuting it in his own mind with the intention, implicit at least, of convincing the attacker of his error. If such a refutation is to be both effective and honest it must first take account of any element of truth contained in the attack, and this will mean carefully rethinking the accepted doctrine without evasion or reservation. In the process the believer may well discover a much deeper personal significance in the teaching he is forced to examine than he had ever expected to find. From then on this aspect of Christianity becomes active in his life, a living, not a dormant, truth.

The other possible effect of an attack on the Faith is to raise a doubt in the believer's own mind. Some part of the Faith suddenly appears as it does to those outside the Church. The believer is forced to ask himself, Do I really believe

this? Does it make sense, or am I living in a
fool's paradise? Such a sudden doubt cannot be
allayed simply by making an act of faith. Certainly an immediate interior assertion of faith
in God's revelation provides the framework
within which understanding may be achieved,
and, incidentally, is reasonable and no evasion
of responsibility, since we know that the evi-
dence for Christianity is not intellectually coer-
cive and that reason alone will not resolve all
difficulties. But if the act of faith is to be a real
supernatural act and not simply a frightened
refusal to face facts lest they prove destructive
of one's spiritual comfort, then it must be ac-
companied by a willingness to use all one's
God-given powers of understanding to obtain a
clearer insight into exactly what it is one is required to believe. Such a search must be under-
taken with humility, that is, with a vivid sense
of one's own spiritual and intellectual limitations and of the enormous areas of ignorance and
mystery that necessarily surround even the most
powerful intellect. But equally it cannot be best
to adopt the attitude exemplified by people who
write to Catholic papers asking, "What must I
believe?" about this or that. Perhaps the writers
of such questions are only trying, quite sensibly,
to get the opinion of competent authorities on
what the Church teaches so that they may understand that teaching more thoroughly and give
free, rational and humble assent to it. But the
impression often given is that the questioner is

merely waiting to be told what to think, quite
literally. Is there not a kind of dishonesty in
proclaiming absolute faith in the Church's
teaching and yet shying away from an unpreju-
diced examination of any one aspect of it? Such
a refusal implies that a Christian is not really
all that sure of the truth of the faith he professes.
Though he will not admit it, he does not look
at doubts or difficulties squarely. He is afraid
that doubts might prove well founded, and then
he would lose the support of the faith on which
he has built his life. Here there is need to dis-
tinguish: to *feel* such a fear of the fallibility of
one's faith is nothing to be ashamed of. It is
often the inevitable result of education and of
the climate of thought in which we live. It is a
temptation like another. To go ahead in spite
of this scarcely admitted fear and force oneself
to probe and dissect and find out the inward-
ness of the Church's teaching requires courage.
It is in itself an act of faith in the Church's guar-
dianship of truth. Such honesty is also, incidentally, most impressive to those outside the
Church. One recent example of this was the
surprise and greatly increased respect for the
Church felt by those observers and journalists
present at the opening sessions of the General
Council who realized that the rulers of the
Church were prepared to look at difficulties
honestly, and when necessary to disagree, instead of (as most people expected) taking refuge
in vague formulae. But whether or not others

are aware of, or helped by, such an example of
personal integrity, the individual is likely to
emerge from the struggle with a deeper, stronger
and more complete faith, and with a stronger
impulse in the living of that faith in daily life.
And since truth is one, though we look at it
from different angles, the single aspect of truth
thus uncovered helps to show up others more
clearly, and to stimulate a desire to extend the
discovery.

In case it might seem that the motives and
benefits of this search for truth are merely intellectual, it is necessary to remember that the
truths in question are those of the Christian
faith. They affect the whole human being and
cannot, of their nature, be confined to the intellect except by doing violence to them, and depriving them of something essential. When
Christ said that he was "the way, the truth,
and the life" he did not mean that he was offering three separate ways of accepting him, like
those manufacturers who propose several different methods of paying for the goods they
offer. To accept the truth of Christ is to accept
himself, to surrender to his transforming grace.
To pursue some aspect of Christian truth is to
attempt to discover Christ more perfectly.

And if it still seems necessary to demonstrate
that such investigations are not just a hobby of
avant-garde Catholic intellectuals of doubtful
orthodoxy, we need only remember St Thérèse
of Lisieux, docile product of the narrowest pos-

sible tradition of orthodox Catholicism. It was her own personal need that drove her to rethink the fundamental Christian virtue of charity, and in so doing to give it new life and motive power not only in her own life but in those of millions of others.

The pursuit of truth requires courage, honesty and diligence. But luckily the process is nothing like so depressing as it sounds. There is no easy way to understanding, but the journey is frequently enlivened by congenial companionship. The grim pioneer discovers that others have travelled the same way and are prepared to come back and escort him along at least part of the road, to point out the view and show him ahead the new country to which he is travelling. He has to make the journey himself, and himself face its dangers and privations, but he is no longer alone. And those who are not too earnest to be amused can find the relief of laughter when they discover that some of their difficulties were quite artificial, that they have been struggling over a sort of doctrinal obstacle-race put up by ill-informed religious teachers of the past.

Many unfortunate laypeople labour for years under the impression that their faith includes all sorts of strange and almost incredible doctrines that are in reality merely the speculations of theologians of the past, who themselves argued from data we now perceive to be incomplete or distorted. The clearing away of such misconceptions, the work of disentangling Christian truth from the opinions of theologians about it, is the task of the General Council. It is also the task—and the comfort—of the ordinary Christian. It may sometimes be hard work, it may require courage to take the plunge, but even on a purely natural level it can lead to release of unnecessary tensions, and to increased confidence and serenity.

This clearance of unnecessary obstacles to understanding is only a part of the whole task of gaining new understanding, but it is a very important, indeed an indispensable part. At this time above all it is the privilege of the ordinary Christian, and his pleasure, to measure up to the unparalleled opportunities offered him in the Church to reach his full stature as a human being, by exercising his God-given intellect on all manner of subjects that concern himself and his contemporaries. In another age, perhaps, other attitudes were understandable and excusable. In our age we could do worse, when confronted with difficulties and challenges in understanding our faith, than to remember the words of Christ to the Apostles, terrified by his appearances in unusual and unnerving circumstances: "It is I. Fear not."

EXPERIENCE AND EXPRESSION IN CHRISTIAN EDUCATION

T HESE essays are the result of a personal effort to rethink many everyday aspects of Christian living in the world. For parents by no means the least important is education. "Our world is a world in a continuous state of becoming, a state in which everything is questioned", writes Cardinal Suenens. "We no longer live in an age where daily lives were solidly framed in tradition, and institutions were there to safeguard values that were never called in question."

In attempting to understand what has happened and what the happenings mean for us, one historical fact takes on importance for all concerned with Christian education. In the disintegration of traditional ideas the way people *lived* Christian ideas and the forms in which these ideas were *expressed* fell apart.

It can happen that a good tradition of living, one basically sound and Christian, may incidentally be expressed in formulae that are much narrower and more rigid than the whole human thing that produced them. This has been the case where Christian education is concerned. In communities, usually compact ones, in which Christian values were taken for granted as the foundation of daily living, the teaching in which these values were expressed could be limited to simple explanations of doctrine and morals, using traditional analogical language. It did not matter if the actual teaching was not well related to daily life, for the relation between doctrine and life was a fact of daily experience. Life itself made up for the inadequacies of expression.

But when daily living must go on in a world where Christian values are no longer taken for granted the old vehicles of teaching become inadequate and may even tend to work against the purpose for which they are used.

This is widely recognized in the Church, and great efforts are made to express Christian truth in ways that mean something to twentieth-century children growing up in a non-Christian world. There is still something lacking, however. Real knowledge does not come with words only. Words are necessary in this world, but are of value only when they crystallize knowledge gained by a mixture (varying widely in its proportions) of experience, intuition, and thought about both these. Even doctrine expressed in clear, supple and meaningful terms remains barren without this.

It seems worth while, therefore, to explore here the possibility that in certain ways current religious teaching, both at home and at school, tends by its nature to reverse the real order of

knowledge. Instead of providing experience, or
the opportunity for experience, and then guid-
ing the children to discover in it the truth that
we want them to know, we simply tell them
things. We try to explain those things as clearly
as possible, and often we try to provide opportunities for the children to exercise the virtues
they have been taught. But it is all back to front.
And the result is that in many cases the teaching
does not in fact lead to real knowledge but only
to a superficial assent to statements unrelated to
life. I don't want to exaggerate the importance
of this. In practice circumstances often put
matters right. Children hear at school teaching
that illuminates their understanding of what
they have experienced at home or among their
friends. Grown-ups suddenly find that the teaching they remember from childhood acquires
meaning from later experience. But all this is
accidental. The fact that so many Christians
settle down to a sincere but superficial practice
of their religion, or gradually abandon it altogether, seems to show that their faith has no roots
in experience, has never been really "known".

At home and at school it does seem as if we
are, without meaning to, forcing the growth of
religious knowledge in an unhealthy way. We
try all the time to explain in childish terms doctrines that only find their full meaning in adult
life. There is no harm in trying to explain complex ideas in simple terms in response to a child's
request—indeed it must be attempted, for the

request implies a background of experience that requires this new knowledge to complete it. But we tend to think that a child *must* be taught the elements of everything before he leaves school. The need for the training of adult Christians is often stressed, but it is always regarded as something *more*, something added on, to improve a structure already complete. This assumption is not surprising, for it is one that governs secular education as well. We talk about "education" and "further education", as if "education" were something that normally finished on leaving school, and was exceptionally continued afterwards. But education is continuous and when it ends the human being stagnates.

This is just as true, and more important, where religious education is concerned. It is natural that parents and teachers, at each stage of schooling, should want to make sure that the pupils have an adequate grasp of the main doctrines of Christianity before the children pass out of their care. This is fine, as long as one has a very clear idea of what constitutes an "adequate grasp" for the individual child at his particular stage of mental and spiritual development. But what too often happens is that, in an attempt to make sure that the children "know their religion", an ability to give clear verbal answers to questions is insisted on. This happens even with teachers who have discarded the use of the Catechism as a normal instrument of teaching. But surely anyone who has lived with children realizes that the ability to give a clear answer is no proof of real understanding. A child who remains tongue-tied or gives wrong or inadequate answers may have failed to grasp what he was taught, but equally he may be struggling for a real understanding which his vocabulary is not yet able to express. The child who gives a good answer may really have understood, but it is possible to remember and recount a lesson in detail without "knowing" what it teaches in the sense described above. The emphasis on the value of clear answers helps to force the pace of religious teaching and to persuade both parents and teachers that the children have received a "good grounding" when all they have received is a collection of unassimilated bits of information, little of which is in any way related to experience. It is true that the wrongness of the system is to a great extent compensated by the understanding the children receive when the personal enthusiasm of the teacher (at home or at school) informs the teaching so that the children share the teacher's experience of his or her religion, by sympathy and intuition. In the hands of a really inspired teacher even Catechism answers can convey knowledge in depth. But most of us are conscious of not being particularly inspired. We are anxious to do a very important job as well as possible, and sometimes it is this very anxiety that makes us require accurate answers as a measure of our achievement. This, of course, links up with the question discussed in the first essay, the relation between a truth and its expression, which, being human, is subject to change. In what sense can a religious "answer" ever be accurate? It should strive to be true, that is, honest and humble, but also personal and related to experience—a much more difficult thing to elicit from a child and one which it may not be wise to require.

It is true that nowadays most teachers realize that learning "parrot-fashion" is of little use. But there is this deeper difficulty connected with the use of words in the teaching of religion. Because words expressing concepts beyond the child's emotional grasp are thrust upon him or her, these are devalued in advance.

I think I may be accused of making a fuss about nothing, and certainly I cannot produce a single case of a child who "lapsed" because his teachers had worn out for him the words that expressed his faith long before he was mature enough to accept them as valid symbols of experience. We are so used to words that we never think about them any more than we think about the air we breathe. But words can become stale, just as the air in a room can. Only it is not as easy to replace an outworn vocabulary as it is to let fresh air into a room.

The Jews had the right idea when they forbade the pronouncing of the name of God. If we were a little more chaste in our use of religious words and phrases their meaning might have more chance of growing in the minds of the children. I have heard children, during Lent, singing a little hymn in which they asked to be allowed "to suffer and to die for thee". This sort of thing is an outrage on the religious integrity of a child. Saints, after a lifetime of striving and loving, hesitate to offer such a prayer and do so with tears of humility—and in private. The growth of the relationship between God and the soul is a delicate thing, easily spoiled, and we trample all over it with trite pieties and forced expressions of emotions that have no place in a child's understanding. One example of this is the constant use of the Holy Name. All the sense of awe, of contact with holiness, of the "special-ness" of the relationship implied by its use in the Liturgy and in private prayer, is destroyed by the chatty, cosy atmosphere in which it is bandied about, until Christ our Lord is reduced to the same level as Father Christmas. "At the name of Jesus every knee shall bow"—but not if its significance has been rubbed away by years of base use. (I know of one adult to whom the phrases of English piety had become so loaded with unreality that he was driven to pray in French in order to achieve the sense that he was being honest with God. Must we teach our children a second language to give them a chance of using words meaningfully? Here is a weapon for the anti-vernacularists!)

Words and phrases that are meaningful at one stage of development can be enforced hypo-crisy at another. To a very small child even the word "love" means nothing. He knows the *thing*, with all his being he knows it—or knows his lack of it. But it is only later that the word and the thing come together in his mind. So even the basic idea, "God loves you", will find a ready understanding only when the idea of love itself has already taken root. The idea of sorrow for sin is another that is easily abused. Real penitence is often of late growth. To suggest the expression of emotions and intentions beyond the child's real capacity is to suggest a lie. Often all the child can manage is a feeling that he has made a muddle of things, and wishes he hadn't. He is not aware of having "offended" God (he probably hasn't), does not think of sin as a *thing*. He has done wrong, that he knows. He wants to be put right. God, he knows, can do that for him. For that he is grateful.

One could go on and on, one could compile a dictionary of words, good, sound words, that have been abused and devalued until their use has become an embarrassment and a stumbling-block in the road instead of part of the paving of the way to heaven.

There is no cut-and-dried answer to these difficulties. It is easy to see what is wrong, much more difficult to suggest practical ways of putting it right. The teacher (at home or at school) who consciously attempts to give the children the sort of experience that can lead to a real "knowledge" of religion will need a generous measure of energy, imagination and courage. The right use of religious words is delicate and difficult.

At this stage in the development of our understanding of catechetics we are still feeling our way, experimenting. But certain lines of approach are worth investigating.

At home the practice of normal Christian virtues by the parents naturally leads the children to practise them too, and then to discover how these things fit into the Christian scheme of life. This very natural development can be consciously turned to account. At school and at home greater emphasis on Scripture gives the beginnings of the experience of growth in understanding the nature of God, by "watching" that understanding grow in the Chosen People. At school, too, group activities for local or wider charities (not just bazaars but personal service) can help, drama can help. At school and in the parish paraliturgical services offer a hopeful field of experiment in the experience of religion. Here the school and/or parish can do what the home cannot do and should not attempt. Communal liturgical life grows out of but transcends the home.

Any or all of these things can give the kind of knowledge we are looking for, experience that can be crystallized into the verbal expressions of doctrine and Christian life. Once words and phrases carry this content of experience they will unlock the door to further experience, they can lead on to the next phase in the development of

2

a Christian personality, and their value will be real and lasting.

We could perhaps learn to exploit the natural crises of growth towards maturity in order to form the religious consciousness. Here is the clue to the *continuing* development of a Christian person, far beyond and beside mere schooling. Even a general realization that Christian education is a lifelong process would be an enormous step forward.

All these possible ways of teaching religion are summed up, ideally, in the full liturgical life of the Church, which takes account of the stages of human life by its sacraments and great feasts. In the Liturgy at its best, devalued words can regain their meaning and their majesty.

Here, ultimately, we can find the answer to both the experience/expression difficulty and the related danger of devaluing the words that express faith. The Liturgy can both express and teach. It can use words as they are meant to be used, though God knows, its more exotic sprouts could well be cut back. Here, in the essential Christian action of worship, we could bring together once more the living of religion and the saying of religion. It is from the Liturgy that we shall develop, if we ever do, a new relation between contemporary Christian life and Christian words. This is not something that can be done overnight. If it is done at all it will take generations. Meanwhile we can at least try to use the

Liturgy as a kind of touchstone of the value and reality of our teaching.

All this may sound too vague and imprecise to be helpful. It is vague because we are dealing with imponderables. It is not possible to give precise instructions for such a reorientation of thought and method. But we have to attempt this reorientation if Christianity is not to become as mummified as Judaism eventually became.

3

"THE GREATEST TREASON"

An article in a Catholic paper, a very sensible article, on the subject of sex education of the young, contained the familiar phrase, "Sex is only a part of life." As it stands, and in the sense intended by the writer, that is a perfectly true statement. We all know about the harm that comes when sex-consciousness, in the sense meant in this quotation, comes to permeate the life of a man or woman to the exclusion of too much else. It is a state of affairs that increasingly worries those responsible for the education of the young, and all sorts of remedies are suggested, between the extremes of those who advocate a "joyous paganism" as a cure for all the world's ills and those who still regard sex as something essentially nasty, the only treatment for which is the respectability overlaid on it by the blessing of church, chapel, or simply of public opinion in legal wedlock.

The first suggestion is touchingly naïve; the second is blasphemous. I venture, with considerable trepidation, and after years of hesitation, to put forward the suggestion that most of the methods of training in purity suggested by sincere Christians must be only partially successful in any real sense, because they are based on the fallacy contained in the phrase quoted: "Sex is only a part of life."

It isn't. One might as well say, "Petrol is only part of driving a car", or "Food and drink are only a part of keeping the body alive". Without petrol you can't drive the car. Without food and drink the body dies. Remove sex from human life and the life is no longer human—nor properly alive.

I wish I could think of another word. I wish we hadn't narrowed down the word "sex" until it means nothing but physical copulation and the ideas and sensations immediately associated with it. What sex should mean, and really is, is the fuel, the driving force, the mainspring of human life—both physical and spiritual. Man was made "in the image of God". "Man and woman he created them." Is there no connection between these two statements? Did God make two sexes just because that was a convenient way for creatures to produce young? Do we really think that God said to himself: "This seems quite a good arrangement, and anyway I can't think of any other"? It needs the apparent irreverence of this simplification to bring out the essential silliness of the purely utilitarian view of sex.

Why, then, did God create two sexes? Why, having done so, did he will that his Son should be born of a virgin? Why has consecrated virginity always been so much revered in the Christian Church?

Surely because the sexual nature of man is a direct expression of something in the divine nature. Isn't this made clear by the virginal conception of the Word made flesh? I have learned from the books of respectable theological writers that it is a tenable opinion that the Virgin Birth was not essential to the Incarnation; in the sense that the Second Person of the Trinity (the Son, Word, or Logos) could have assumed to union with himself a human nature conceived in the ordinary way from the action of two human parents.

But was it not in a real sense essential to the Incarnation to show that man's sexual nature is derived directly from God? We have said so often the words "conceived by the Holy Ghost, born of the Virgin Mary", we are so used to the pictures of the Annunciation, that we lose sight of what it actually means: God uniting himself with the physical process of conception, God himself using directly the power which he normally delegates to a human being.

What of consecrated virginity? It has so often been taken by non-Christians—and, unhappily, by many Christians—as a proof that, for all the lip-service paid to the sanctity of marriage, the Church really regards sex as unclean, and reserves its admiration for those who have renounced it.

We also notice that the Old Testament lays emphasis on the fact that all engaged in the worship of God must carefully "cover their nakedness". Marital intercourse was considered to unfit a man for religious duties for a specified period. Doesn't all this bear out the idea that Christianity, in its Scriptures and in its practice, regards sex as essentially degrading?

To go back to the Old Testament again for a minute: The prophet Ezekiel[1] records that in his vision of God he saw "the form of what looked like a man", seated on something like a throne. "Above the loins this form looked like flashing metal, but from what seemed to be his loins downwards I had the impression of fire." This symbol emphasizes the sexlessness of the one God. In describing this vision the seer gets rid of the crudities of the contemporary pagan religions, which conceived the power of God in sexual terms and attempted to use this power in essentially "magical" rites. These sexual rites, so sternly denounced by the Hebrew prophets, were intended to compel the power of divine fertility to become effective on earth through the agency of ritual sexual intercourse.

The idea is familiar. The Jewish tradition was at pains to contradict it; and this was particularly necessary because the germ of truth contained in the idea had been completely overlaid

[1] See the article by Fr Joseph Bourke, O.P., "From Temple to Heavenly Court", *Life of the Spirit* (April 1962).

by the crude magical interpretation given to it.

The mistake of the pagan cults is the same mistake made today by those who teach that sex is only a part of life. The old religions, perceiving dimly that sexual power and fertility in general must have their source in the Creator, argued back from the physical processes of human sex, which seemed to them the whole of sex, and attributed these, more or less "spiritualized", to their divinities. The Jewish tradition said: No. That is all wrong. God is not sexual. We will make this clear by separating all physical reminders of sex from the ritual worship of God. But, sexual power *comes from God*. Therefore a large family of healthy children is a sign of God's blessing. Therefore, also, marital faithfulness is important; human sexual powers are not to be lightly used. Above all, the Holy People must not have intercourse with the daughters of the uncircumcised. In other words, human sex is holy, and is a manifestation of the power of God; but we must do nothing that might suggest even remotely that God is subject to the limitations of his own creation.

But whatever God creates is an expression of himself. If human sexuality is an expression of his abounding creative power—a creative power which makes because it loves and loves because it makes—then it is clearly something essential, not something accidental, to human nature. It is not something added on to show authorship, like the artist's signature on his picture. It is, to pursue the metaphor a little further, the "style" of the painting, the individual touch, the unmistakable expression of personality that makes one say, "I know who painted that; only one person could have done it like that."

In this context (to return to the question that started this particular bit of exploration) consecrated virginity makes complete sense. It shows, as nothing else could, that we acknowledge the link between human sexuality and the divine creativity. Human beings endowed with normal sexual powers lay aside the physical use of them in order to worship their Author with all the powers of their (fully sexual) nature. The existence of the state of religious virginity is not, then, to be regarded as a condemnation of the physical use of sex. It is rather a constant witness to the fact that sex is something more than physical; that it is, in fact, the meeting-point of the spiritual and the physical in man. It is the proof that this slightly ridiculous creature who reproduces himself by the crudely physical union of two bodies is, in that very act, in touch with and fired by the transcendent, completely unphysical, glory of the God who is love.

But the purpose that sparked off these questions and investigations was not an abstract desire to explore the nature of human sexuality, but the very practical and urgent need to find an effective way of training young Christians in the virtue of purity, i.e., of relating their sexual life—and we do not need to be told nowadays that children *have* a sexual life—to God its Author.

There are various ways of doing it, and some of them are very effective if one reckons success by how well the products of these methods achieve continence. Nearly every book for parents, every manual of the Christian life, contains rule-of-thumb methods for coping with sexual temptations or sins by means of careful examination of conscience and constant prayer, combined with the cultivation of Alternative Activities.

But there is another point of view: the need for continence is not self-evident. In one of Dorothy Sayers' novels there is a remark by her hero, Lord Peter Wimsey (to my mind the ideal humanist): "As for the gift of continence," he says, "I wouldn't have it as a gift." That is not just a tasteless joke. It is perfectly reasonable. Why should he, or any other human being, desire continence? Because God says sexual intercourse outside marriage is wrong? True enough; but not a sufficient answer. It is very understandable that non-Christians should take leave to doubt our flat statement that God has laid down such strict conditions for what is potentially the most joyful of all purely human experiences. (The fact that it is frequently a squalid, miserable and frustrating experience is neither here nor there; no-one *expects* his or hers to be like that.) And although our children are given a different point of view their own instincts, as they grow up, and almost all outside influences, seem to contradict our moral statements. This contradiction is reinforced by the natural and necessary tendency of adolescents, in their efforts to develop as human beings, to push against their parents.

So they need to know why the Church has given this restrictive report of God's ideas on the subject of sex. They need a "reason" that appeals not only to the head but to the heart also, to the whole human being in fact. Too often we try to force our growing children to accept a ban on sexual intercourse before marriage by methods which actually contradict the real reason for the prohibition.

It is not so very difficult to build up in the mind of a child a series of "conditioned reflexes" which make him or her react to sexual suggestions of all kinds with strong feelings of guilt and repulsion. This method was once almost universally, and is still frequently, adopted by conscientious Christian teachers and parents. It can be extremely effective in the sense explained above, and has been used in the formation of saints (notably St Thérèse of Lisieux, who "never felt at home in her body"), and because it "works" and is associated with the lives of so many saints it has acquired a sort of halo. Nowadays we do not usually try to produce the extreme repulsion to all things physical that made St Mary Euphrasia, for instance, refuse to see a doctor when she developed a tumour in the breast. But we still use this method of sex education. We use it whenever we show unreasonable (to the child) anger or repulsion to a small child who is found exploring his body in what we think is an "immodest" way. We use it when we protest or even giggle rather hysterically at the crude remarks or gestures of children with reference to their physical functions, or when we denounce them in outraged tones as "disgusting". We use it when we describe certain actions and people as "nasty", without explanation. What happens to a young man or woman so trained when desire, after all, gets the upper hand, is very "nasty" indeed. Their reactions have very little to do with true contrition, and may easily produce a state of mind that feels itself permanently shut off from grace, so that one "might as well be hanged for a sheep as a lamb".

Let us also consider the possible results of such training when the victim marries. It is useless to tell our children that marriage is holy and blessed by God if their whole upbringing has conditioned them (not by precise words, but in hints, atmosphere and feeling, and by what is *not* said) to associate sex with guilt and fear and misery.

Two results can follow. In one case the young couple discover that sex is delightful. But they have always felt it as wrong, in a real and basic way, *even though* they have been taught the Christian doctrine on marriage. So their delight becomes a guilty delight, subtly but really separated from their religious life. (I am discussing the children of Christians.) The other possible result is that the fears and guilt actually spoil the experience of sex for both. This leads to an essentially imperfect marriage. They may surmount this and remain together in love and trust, offering their unhappiness to God in patient love. Or one or other may seek outside marriage what he or she cannot find inside it, tacitly overthrowing, when too late, the ideas that caused the damage. Or they may stick it out in stoic bitterness and pass on to their children their own resentment and disappointment. The effect on the children of the parents' unsatisfactory sex life is the psychiatrists' happy hunting ground.

There is, thank God, a third possibility. The couple realize what is wrong, and gradually and painfully struggle free of their false consciences, to recover, at last, the harmony with each other and with God of which they had been robbed.

(In parenthesis, I am inclined to think that one reason for the fact that the majority of canonized saints were consecrated virgins is connected with this method of inculcating the virtue of purity. The physical use of sex becomes so much associated with evil that marriage would produce a conflict with the religious consciousness that must make a peaceful relationship with God impossible. The same sexual powers channelled into the worship and service of God alone lead to peace and fulfilment, and flower in the lovely lives of people like St Gertrude, St John of the Cross and thousands of others.)

There is another solution to the problem of training in continence. It is not nearly so "effective" in practice, but it is widely used by good non-Christians and by Christians who have realized the dangers of the traditional method.

It is based on commonsense sex instruction of a positive and encouraging kind, supported by sensible explanations of the need for stable family life in bringing up babies. Non-Christians shore up the shaky bits of this rampart by appeals to "self-respect" as a motive for preserving continence before marriage. Christians add to this the Christian teaching on the indissolubility of marriage, plus an explanation of why "hard cases make bad law". This teaching is intended as a defence of the Church's strictness in the matter of divorce; and in defence of purity before marriage they offer an improved version of the "self-respect" theme: the idea that one should preserve for the person one will love in marriage the act that is the fullest expression of that love.

I say that this method is less "effective" because it does not provide any "built-in" safeguard in the form of a conditioned repulsion from sexual images and suggestions. Therefore the young man or woman who has been taught in this way is more likely to succumb to violent emotions that sweep away, temporarily at least, the sensible arguments that commanded the assent of the reason alone. In fact, this nowadays accepted second method errs not in what it does but in what it leaves out. All the teaching I have summarized above is perfectly good and right as far as it goes (apart from the "self-respect" business, which is a hidden throw-back to the sex-is-nasty conditioning). But it is surely quite secondary. There appears to be something wrong with a presentation of the Christian attitude to sex that shows marriage *only* as a sensible provision of Almighty God's for the social welfare of the race.

The last temptation is the greatest treason;
To do the right deed for the wrong reason.

Eliot's rather trite little couplet neatly expresses a terrifying truth.

I can't help wondering whether it isn't less evil for our children to succumb to the temptations of the flesh than to stand against them because they are afraid of their instincts: afraid and guilty for reasons they don't understand because they aren't "reasons". It seems possible that the young man or woman who has experienced the joy and sorrow, the exaltation and humiliation of a love affair, is more likely to come in the end to a true understanding of God's purpose in making humans sexual than one who has resisted temptation by a combination of unreasoning repulsion and selfconscious righteousness. I am not, of course, saying that it is a good thing to have casual affairs, or a bad thing to preserve physical integrity, even at the cost of great agony of mind. Only that continence is not necessarily the same thing as purity; and also that incontinence does not necessarily imply a lack of moral sensibility; it may rather indicate the reverse.

It seems, then, that I reject a training which is not a training of mind and will and emotions but rather a deliberate conditioning of unconscious reactions. I reject as insufficient a "normal, sensible" sex training, even in a context of sincere Christian goodness and piety. What, then, *do* I want?

Something very risky and very delicate; something with no certainty of success if you count success in percentages; something that lays the individual open to every kind of sorrow and suffering and exploitation. A training which aims at producing a human being sensitive, according to individual capacity, to all kinds of goodness and beauty; and therefore to all kinds of evil and ugliness. It is a training that runs the constant risk of failure because it provides no automatic safeguards against contrary influences from outside, only the safeguard of the soul's own desire for goodness, expressed in prayer. It is a training, in fact, that depends entirely on the response of the individual to God. It is a training that hopes and prays for that lovely and terribly rare result: a man or woman who is able to love. Is it worth risking so much? Wouldn't it be better to stick to the safe and tried methods

that have for generations produced good practising Christians and many saints? Isn't it pre-
sumptuous to try to improve upon the careful
moral cultivation of so many centuries? I don't
know. I really don't. But I am haunted by a
possibility.

Supposing there were a baby who was taught
from the beginning to treat beautiful things
with love and care. Supposing he were not
allowed to tear daisies to bits, but gently and
lovingly taught to hold, smell and look at them
without hurting them. Suppose he were encouraged, as he grew, to touch animals and flowers,
books and other babies very gently and lovingly,
to look and enjoy but *not spoil*. Suppose he
learnt this not by being punished when he was
rough but by being personally helped to treat
things in the right way. Suppose that as soon as
he began to understand simple ideas he were
constantly shown how beautiful things are, and
encouraged to look and handle but *never spoil*.

Suppose he were encouraged to make lots of
things, and much praised when he did. Suppose
that from very early years he learnt that God is
someone who wants him to enjoy all manner of
things, and himself to make as many things as
he is able; but never, never to spoil things. (Not
even a bird's egg or a "weed".) Suppose he learnt
that it is good to share things we like, because
they are not ours but are lent by God who made
and loves others as he made and loves us. Suppose he learnt, for instance, to lay a table beauti-

fully and enjoy its beauty, and to regret the
accident that spilt jam on the cloth because it
spoils the beauty (but never because it's *bad* to
spill jam).

Suppose he learnt, soon, that God made his
body, and other people's; made *all* of it. And
that it's lovely and exciting and interesting.
Suppose he were told that God has wonderful
plans for human bodies that a child cannot completely understand yet, but that he should look
after his body very carefully, and one day he will
understand. Suppose that if, for instance, he developed a habit of playing about with his genital
organs no-one was shocked but he was simply
told, firmly but gently, that this is not a good
idea because they are very special and should
not be treated as toys. Suppose that this did not
remain negative, but led to unselfconscious discussions about his body, and about babies, and
all his questions, then and every time, were
answered clearly and simply and fully, according
to his age and capacity. Suppose that the whole
of his instruction in sex were given with some
of the infectious enthusiasm that we normally
reserve for descriptions of a successful holiday
or a new car. Suppose that he grew up to understand that God had made him able to share in
his own divine life of creation, that all God's
gifts were for his use, but each in its own right
way; to use and *not to spoil*. And that he, like
God, could make things; not just things you can
see, like paintings or cakes or a garden or a

wooden box, but things you can't see, like goodness and kindness and courage and love. And
that we must *share* these things, because, seen
or unseen, we make them by God's power, not
our own. We do not possess anything, except in
a purely legal sense.

Suppose that as he grew he began to feel
changes in his body and strange new ideas and
emotions, and learnt to welcome them because
they were a sign that in him God's power of
creation (of things, and of ideas and of goodness)
was developing. Suppose that by now he had a
very clear idea that sex is holy because it is
God's power working in us. Suppose that he
began to learn, as he matured, that marriage is
the living sign of Christ's love for his Church;
that when married people use their dedicated
and sanctified bodies to express their love for
each other they are also expressing God's love
for human souls; and that since God's "expressions" are not just empty words these two people
are actually *making love*. The real thing: God's
love.

And suppose that he understood the holiness
of virginity, and knew that it was not a rejection
of something bad but a consecration of those
same powers to the service of God in a different
kind of love-making. Suppose that, praying a lot,
he gradually came to know what was God's will
for him. And suppose that in the years of his
growing up (whichever course he finally followed) he felt the stirring of the flesh not as a

threat but as a challenge, a proof both of his human dignity and of his human weakness and need of God's help, and it became an occasion of prayer.

Suppose that he could see the shape of a pretty girl and praise God for it, and not be afraid of the quickening of his pulse but accept it as natural and good, knowing what it is for and yet not carried away by it. And suppose that, if he found his senses troubling him too much he could take precautions against too much excitement, by prayer and hard work, without getting into a panic or feeling guilty. Suppose that he really fell in love, and was glad and enjoyed it, and yet, having learnt that creation is to be used and enjoyed but not spoiled, he showed reverence for the body of the girl as he had learnt to reverence his own, and all other good things.

Suppose that if he did fall into sexual sin he could be sorry and ashamed and seek forgiveness, but not feel branded for ever by an irrevocable action. (A fairly serious spiritual scar can be left on a sensitive personality by sexual sin, because it is so fundamental—but there is no need to aggravate the wound artificially.)

Suppose that, then or later, he met a girl who understood, or was prepared to learn to understand with him, what sex is for and what Christian marriage really means. And they were married. And neither of them had any feelings of guilt, nor did they regard sex as merely "natural", just a bit of legitimate fun, the jam on the bread of the daily routine. Suppose they knew it was fun and could laugh, and knew it was delightful and enjoyed it, and knew it was love and loved it, and knew it was holy and reverenced it, and knew it was also much bigger than they could understand and were awed by it . . .

Imagine the kind of children they might have. Imagine the life that would spread out from them like ripples, and "make love" for all kinds of people.

Or suppose he didn't marry. Suppose he used the creative power within him to serve God some other way—as a priest or a religious, or in some "secular" calling. He would still be "making love", because he would know where love came from.

I have written only about a boy's growing up, but of course the principle is equally valid for a girl, though the problems are different.

Perhaps this is all a futile dream. Perhaps it is safer to build ramparts and get inside them. Not that they seem to be so very effective. Young people get fed up with the walls, and one fine night they are up and over. And there is another drawback about living inside a fortress: it doesn't encourage neighbourliness. One is too busy keeping the defences in order to have time to bother about someone else's troubles. Let him build his own little castle.

There are such depths and heights to be explored in discovering the meaning of Christian

marriage that to try to do so here would be
ridiculous. I have assumed a realization of some
of this, and of many other things. I am concerned here simply to make a plea for the throw-
ing-down of barriers, for a training that would
encourage young men and women to go out to
face all their experiences with no defences but
three: faith, hope, charity. But the greatest of
these is charity. And the best method of defence
is attack; the kind of attack that is indicated by
the defencelessness of the child in the manger
and the man on the cross.

Before I am entirely condemned, consider
what quality it is that we find most attractive in
another human being—in the saints we read
about or the friends we know. Isn't it the quality
of responsiveness, of sympathy? The man or
woman who comes up to every experience—a
flower or a baby or a blind man, or death—with
open hands and heart; the one who seems to
experience your experience, who is racked by
your sorrow or exalted by your love affair; who
cannot see suffering without wanting to put it
right, or joy without wanting to enhance it.
Isn't this the kind of person we turn to, whether
it be a Francis of Assisi or an Elizabeth of Hun-
gary or the woman next door or the man at the
garage?

Has this got anything to do with training in
purity? I think it has.

4

HOW MANY CHILDREN?

A N awful lot of nonsense is written about large families. Members of the Eugenics Society, advocates of artificial contraception, and many warm-hearted but woolly-headed people (all honour to them) see the squalor, destitution and premature ageing of the women in certain countries, notably Catholic ones, and conclude that since large families are so often to be found where such conditions exist they are therefore the cause of the conditions; with the corollary that it is all the Church's fault for forbidding artificial birth control.

On the other hand, you meet Catholics who talk as if Catholic mothers were failing in their duty if they did not produce a baby a year, regardless of their health or their husband's income. It is also said that large families are, *ipso facto*, happier, jollier, less selfish, more pious, etc., etc.

It is necessary to consider how much truth there may be behind these exaggerations before one can helpfully suggest what might be the Christian attitude to the question of how big a family should be. (I am not concerned here to discuss birth control in its controversial aspects.

This is a very important matter, but I am purposely avoiding the issue here. The controversy is basically about *means* of controlling fertility. My interest here is not in "how" but in "whether" and "why".)

How much truth is there in the idea that where the influence of the Catholic Church is strong there are always large families, and therefore dirt, destitution, disease and oppressed womenfolk? Quite a lot if you recognize that in this context the influence of the Church in certain countries sometimes means the general attitude of a wrongly or badly trained clergy, an attitude based on a "textbook" moral theology unrelated to the living words of the Gospel and a proper pastoral understanding of human nature and human problems. It is no secret that such priests do still exist, especially, but not only, in certain areas of some of the Latin countries. And poverty can be a vested interest of civil governments also, under certain circumstances— not to mention criminal organizations; but their members will usually be "nominal" Catholics only. This is the state of affairs that drives men like Danilo Dolci to refuse the Christian "label" in connection with the struggle for social reform and better living conditions for the oppressed.

There seems to be a tragic distortion of true Christian morality when clergy are found who insist that artificial contraception is morally wrong but seldom point out with any conviction that defrauding labourers of their wages and oppression of the poor are among the sins that "cry to heaven for vengeance"; and that these sins on the part of those in power are what produce conditions in which flourish those "sins" into which desperately poor people can easily slip.

Among these sins is the misuse of the marriage right. Sex has been described as "the cocktail of the poor", and indeed desperate and despairing poverty, which makes even drunkenness a rare privilege, find its only oblivion, its only pleasure, in sex. That, and not the lack of artificial contraception *as such*, is the reason for the swarming families of the destitute. Destitution, which is not the same thing as poverty, breeds its own kind of animality, and there is an unpleasant kind of smugness in regarding this as unimportant provided the more obvious sins are avoided.

All this seems to suggest that those who blame squalor and poverty on large families are confusing cause with effect. Artificial limiting of these families would not solve the basic problems, either economically or morally. There would be fewer children to starve, but also fewer children growing up to earn, and an ageing population is more of a problem than one with a proper proportion of young people who, *given the opportunity*, could earn a living and support both themselves and those past work. And, while no-one in his senses would dare pass judgement of sin on those who, in circumstances akin to those of prisoners under torture, make use of artificial contraceptives, it is not hard to see that *when their use is imposed by fear* it can gradually eat away the general moral sense of a community. All this applies not only to such glaring examples as Sicily, but also in some degree to families in the poor districts of industrial cities in Great Britain. The same kind of conditions, bred by the same kind of causes (though much less severe) produce the same results: depression, hopelessness, irresponsible misuse of sex as a cheaply available respite from squalor, leading not only to the procreation of unwanted children but to a selfish and absolutely un-Christian attitude to marriage. But apparently this state of affairs is all right in the eyes of many Catholics provided the couples concerned do not artificially limit their families.

Then there is the other point of view: the view of those people who regard the procreation of numerous children as essentially virtuous, and who are sure that members of large families are necessarily happier, more cheerful, more diligent and unselfish. There is a lot of truth in this idea also. Couples who have a lot of children because they want a lot of children, and not because they didn't prevent them being born, do achieve a unity and warmth in their marriage, and a degree of unselfishness, of forgetfulness of self, which is unusual. And children brought up in a group of others are forced, in the absence of numerous servants, to wait on themselves and each other at an early age, to sacrifice their own pleasures to those of the others, and usually to help their parents a good deal if the work of the household is to be done at all. This often makes them early into independent and responsible people, and they get into the habit of putting other people's needs before their own. But those who notice and applaud such phenomena frequently do not realize that these good things do not happen automatically.

A large number of children can lead not to unity between the parents but to a gradual estrangement. The wife sometimes becomes more and more absorbed in the children, the husband feels she puts him second, and he takes to spending more time with his friends. The wife feels that he is not pulling his weight with her increasing burden of work and is not sufficiently interested in the children who are her life. She retaliates by becoming more and more immersed in the children, she takes little trouble about her appearance, and never has time to share her husband's interests. And so it goes on.

In a large family there are certainly ample opportunities for unselfishness, but there is also greater scope for quarrelling, bickering, jealousy. This can be a good thing. Sooner or later everyone has to learn to live with other people whose company he finds occasionally, or even permanently, uncongenial. To begin early to learn to adjust to the moods of others, and control one's own, is an advantage. But this adjustment is not automatic. It requires positive, and sustained, help from the parents. If the parents fail, culpably or not, to give this help the children grow up in a jungle of unchecked ill-temper, rapacity and ruthless competition. So it can happen all too easily that children of big families, far from growing up unselfish and cheerful, can learn to grab, to be always on the watch to snatch an advantage. Again, the extra work and absence of luxuries that are often the condition of having a large family can breed a permanent resentment. The children feel they are treated as unpaid servants, they must forgo normal treats and comforts because, without consulting them, their parents chose to have more children than other couples they know. They do not learn to accept small privations cheerfully. On the contrary, they resolve that they will be as thoroughly selfish as they can be once they leave the prison house. They usually have only one or two children themselves, if they marry at all. The reason is not far to seek: the work and deprivations remained negative; they were never seen as acts of love.

Let no-one think that it is easy for children to accept harder work and fewer comforts, any more than it is for grown-ups. When their home conditions are contrasted with those of other children met at school or in the neighbourhood the immediate reaction is likely to be one of resentment. It needs constant explanation, support and encouragement from the parents, long and patient education in Christian values, to make such unpleasant things seem worth while. Even when the parents see the greater good that makes work and privations worth while, the children remain to be convinced. If they are not so convinced the results will be bad, not good.

What, then, is the Christian approach to these complex problems, between the extremes?

The Christian idea of marriage is one of loving service; service of God, and, in God, of the partner and the children. This rules out the limiting of families (by whatever method) for purely selfish reasons. It also rules out the irresponsible procreation of children regardless of the health and temperament (not to mention income) of either partner. One hears a lot about the burden of the mother. It is often forgotten that in some cases the burden of a large family may bear hardest on the father. This can happen if, for instance, the mother is healthy and of a resilient temperament while her husband is the worrying sort. His, after all, is the burden of supporting the growing family. In some cases it may be more virtuous, more unselfish, for a couple to try to have fewer children. This may involve considerable sacrifice on both sides. The self-control needed by those who use the "rhythm" method of controlling fertility is never easy when a couple really love each other. For the wife the decision may mean that she must do without another baby for which she craves. Some women do have a real longing for one more baby, and this need must be balanced against the burden it may impose on the husband.

When Catholics, especially, discuss the advisability of having a large family, they naturally consider the health of the parents. But they usually mean physical health only. If the mother is obviously sickly or overtired, or the husband not fit for full-time work, the reasons for limiting the family are obvious. But too often the question of mental or even spiritual health is never raised. Yet it can be more important. A woman with comparatively poor physical health, provided she is not actually ill, may well make a good job of rearing a family because she is easygoing, placid, patient, optimistic by nature. She will not let housework "get on top of her", she will sit down and relax even if there *is* a pile of ironing waiting to be done. Her neighbours will say she is a slut, but her children will be cheerful and contented even if dirty. A man may be obliged by ill-health to be frequently off work. But if he is able to accept a lower standard of living without working himself into a nervous dither because there is no TV aerial on the roof and his front door needs painting he will make an excellent father. On the other hand the physically sturdy woman who, for whatever reason, is in a state of "nerves", natters at the children, grumbles at her husband, and jumps at every loud noise, is not a fit person to manage a large family. The man who, though healthy and financially secure, is a cringing target for the

lewd jokes of his companions if he has more than
two children, will not give his wife the support
she needs in bringing up the children. He will
resent their presence. The man who feels inadequate either as husband or father, and lies
awake at night worrying—needlessly perhaps—
about his past or possible failures is not, in the
full sense, "healthy" either.

These random examples show that when
health is in question as a factor in deciding on
the number of children it is the health of the
marriage that matters. It is not enough to have
sufficient money, decent housing, reasonable
physical health. It is the health of the marriage
relationship that makes the right or wrong
setting for a family. It must not be forgotten that
in many cases the birth of children can be the
means of healing an unhealthy marriage, but on
the other hand that extra baby may be the last
straw that breaks the shaky marriage. Certainly,
a large family is not such a cure-all. On such a
complex subject it is a mistake to lay down the
law with the blind assumption of infallibility
that some Catholics assume.

The ordinary healthy couple starting out into
marriage as Christians have two points of view
presented to them. There is that of many of their
contemporaries outside the Church who regard
children as a lovely and normal "extra", of whom
there must not be more than two or three lest
they interfere too much with the personal life of
the parents. This is not always as selfish as it

sounds. If you regard marriage as basically a relationship of two people only, with children as
optional extras, then it is reasonable to limit the
number of children to one that can be reared
with the virtual certainty that they will not
strain either the finances, the health or the
nerves of their parents. Such parents will usually
tell you that they limit the number for the children's own sake: "We couldn't give them the sort
of life we want for them if we had more" is the
formula. Sometimes this formula is a sincere expression of belief. Sometimes it is a routine
cover-up. In saying this I am not saying such
couples are wrong to limit their families; they
may have real and convincing reasons for doing
so. But they are looking at the whole matter from
a wrong point of view.

The other view is the Christian one which
regards children as one of the purposes of marriage, through which the other purpose—the
fulfilment, physical, mental and spiritual, of the
couple in and by each other—will normally be
accomplished.

In practice—and this is a matter of simple ob-
servation—the Christian ideal produces happier,
more balanced, more mature human beings.
This needs saying, because we are accustomed to
regard the laws of God as arbitrary inventions of
Almighty—as if God intended to keep us in order
like children in school. In fact, they are a well-
balanced recipe for happiness, and if any in-
gredients are left out or skimped the cake will

be unappetizing and indigestible. But however firmly we believe that God's law is right and best, we are all up against a very strong tide of opinion that equates happiness with abundance of leisure and pleasure of a rather stereotyped kind. A certain amount of each is essential, though the amount must inevitably vary widely, and a sane Christian life includes both. ("Wearing myself out for my children/husband/parents" is not necessarily a Christian way to behave. It may be a way of managing people by emotional black-mail, or it may be due to an unconscious feeling of guilt.) But happiness is not the result of these. Happiness is an inevitable by-product of doing God's will (even in people who do not know that it is his will) in whatever vocation, and rearing a family brings a lot of it. On the other hand, the couple who plan for happiness, ruling out for its sake the "extra" children, may end by missing it altogether.

At this point, then, it seems that having a large family does not necessarily lead to squalor, is not necessarily virtuous, but is a good way for a Christian couple to fulfil their vocation. This is not to say that the best thing is to have as many babies as "happen". A healthy couple with a cheerful pious outlook and a reasonable income can do it, and make a huge success of it. These are some of the happiest families you can find. But it is often more sensible to try to leave a reasonable interval between the children for the sake of the mother's health—not to mention the

3

father's. I have purposely said *try* to limit, *try* to leave an interval.

It is perfectly in accordance with the Church's present teaching to avoid conception for serious reasons by the use of the infertile period, and generally this works excellently. The method of determining ovulation by recording the basal temperature is simple and reliable. It has brought release from fear to many anxious couples, and helped to save marriages near breaking. Continuing research is making this method of controlling family size more certain and less complicated, and other methods of determining ovulation are being tested. It seems likely that determination of the fertile period will become increasingly a matter of course, whether to control family size, space the children out, or make conception more likely when the wanted baby is elusive. But it is possible to make a mistake in reading the temperature chart, though this becomes unlikely with practice. Also, it is of the essence of the marriage contract that the sexual need of either partner must be paramount; so that it may happen that the "risk" of another baby must be run rather than force one or other partner to an occasion of sin. And so there may be another baby coming that was not "planned for". This happens, too, to couples who use artificial contraceptives; in fact, they are not as completely "safe" as their advocates would like us to think, or as they may become after further research.

In the case of non-Christians the attitude to this may be one of resentment, leading perhaps in the end to acceptance and a surprised pleasure. But this can never be the Christian attitude. Christians must take reasonable thought for the future, must take into account such things as health and wealth (or lack of them), and make their prudent decisions. But they know that all such decisions are made under God; and that in the last resort all that matters is to do his will, so that if their plans are overruled, then God is showing them his will in a more direct way. The "unplanned" baby—or, more sadly, the un-planned lack of babies—is a part of God's plan for this particular family.

Doing the will of God does not necessarily mean feeling happy about the form it takes. Acceptance is a matter of will, not emotions. Wholehearted acceptance of what God sends is perfectly compatible with dread of the burden he seems to be imposing, even with waves of panic fear at the thought of what lies ahead. To accept what God sends does not confer immunity from normal human pains and fears; it only makes them innocuous to the soul, which re-mains unshakeably attached to the divine will, however "crazy" its manifestations may seem. In course of time the soul's serenity may seep through to the emotions also.

To have a big family can be a marvellous thing; it can bring joy and satisfaction and warmth. It can develop in the whole family the

best of which they are capable. But we are thinking of a *human* family, and the thing that makes
a human being is the power to choose. There is
an understandable tendency among those who
have authority in the Church to want to limit
the choices available to Catholics, lest they choose
wrongly. They want to protect Christ's flock by
enclosing it in a safe sheepfold with high walls.
But we are not sheep in that sense. The Church
needs people who do good because they choose
to, not because they have no real alternative.
Such a "good" is not a moral good because it
lacks the condition required for a moral quality:
choice.

Many honest non-Christians share the desire
to deny to human beings the power of choice.
They do it by denying its existence. If God
exists, they say, how can he be good if he gives
his creatures the power of choice, lets them make
disastrous choices? Would you let your child
choose if a wrong choice could ruin his life?
That is the question they put. The answer is,
must be: If the right choice means the chance
of something sufficiently valuable then the risk
is worth while, however terrifying. If a human
parent can find the courage to say that, then we
must not insult almighty God by attempting to
deny to Christians, however humble, the power
of choice with which he has endowed them.
They may choose wrongly; probably, they often
will. Whatever the risks, however high the proportion of failures, to choose is nobler, is more

human, than to be the passive victims of a fate we cannot control.

Where the size of a family is concerned, the power to choose effectively is a comparatively recent development. (I am not speaking here of couples who decide—again a choice—on complete continence, whether permanently or for a limited period. This is a special vocation, and a valuable one, but it is not a solution that can be imposed on most couples; if it is to be holy it must be the response to a definite and exceptional call. Otherwise it is disastrous. I am not leaving it aside because I think it unimportant, but because it is a separate and very big subject, one not to be included in the general subject of family size.) There has been and still is a tendency among some Catholics to think that it is better for us not to be able to control the size of our families really efficiently, even when the reasons for doing so are morally valid. They are so conscious of the danger of mixed motives, of selfishness masquerading as good sense and prudence, that they would deny to ordinary people the power to choose when to have a child.

These dangers are real. It is easy to take un-Christian values for granted, easy to overvalue material security, easy to confuse timidity and prudence. But the denial of the power to choose is no solution. This protective urge is no doubt very natural—but it is not supernatural. In this century when the laity is at last coming of age it is time to be clear that in this matter, as in

others, we are not minors. We are responsible
before God for the choices we make, and no-one
has the right to deny us the choice, if God has
given it to us.

The usual Catholic reaction to a home full
of children is, "What a wonderful family." The
assumption is that any big family is "wonderful". It can be. It should be. But it is not an
absolute good. Its full goodness will have a
chance to develop if it is the result of a free
choice, of human wills moving in rhythm with
the will of God, consciously helping to carry out
one small part of his design.

5

"MY LOVE HERSELF ADORNING"

THE time when saints and sages thundered against the wickedness of women who adorned themselves with jewellery, embroidery, bright colours or, worst of all, paint on their faces, is over. It is not hard to see why they adopted this attitude, in an inherited pagan system of social morality in which a respectable woman was a submissive and silent breeder of children and organizer of the household, and only "bad" women made themselves conspicuous by adorning either their persons or their minds. It took a long time before pious Christians could consider women as persons. They had, of course, immortal souls—one was obliged to admit that—but this was felt to be a big concession. Let them not therefore presume. Their only hope of salvation lay in absolute submission, hiddenness, in constant good works and in being as dreary as possible to look at. For woman was, after all, responsible for the miserable state of the human race. Woman must bear for ever the guilt of Eve. She was still a menace to the salvation of men, a source of temptation even to the elect, and as such must be disciplined and made as inconspicuous as possible. The frenzied attacks on the female sex of some eminent Christians in the early centuries of the Christian era raise irrepressible suspicions about their own state of mind, and this almost hysterical fear of women—really of sex—was one of the things that helped to debase (or keep debased) for so long the state of matrimony. The sacramental nature of marriage was felt during most of the "Middle Ages" (using the term imprecisely) to be merely conferring a permissive blessing on a union basically corrupt. Virginity was the only real way out, marriage was a necessary concession to the weakness of human nature, and its holiness consisted in the pious rearing of a family, for which the sex act was, unfortunately, indispensable.

No wonder human nature rebelled against this distortion and attempted, in the concept of courtly love, to show that physical love was good, and the woman who was its object worthy of respect, service, even of something approaching worship. It was suggested by one contemporary writer (whether in earnest or with his tongue in his cheek is still disputed) that true love in marriage was impossible, even immoral, because love must be free, or it is not love, and the marriage contract ruled out freedom.

Irrational as these ideas were, and destined to end in a blind alley, they did do much to change the attitude of Christian civilization to married women. (Religious women, however, for a long time had held positions of responsibility and gained respect, though their status waned towards the close of the Middle Ages.) In its repudiation of the value of religious virginity, and its consequent need to revalue marriage, the Protestant Reformation did more. It is noticeable that those of Donne's love-poems which were written to his wife do not differ in tenderness and passion from those to more temporary companions, and seem to show, if anything, a greater depth of feeling.

Although in the Catholic Church there continued to be a strong tradition that still regarded marriage as a very poor second-best to religious virginity, there was a gradual change in the general attitude. St Francis de Sales regarded it as right and proper for a young woman to dress attractively according to her station in life, since unless she was intended (the verb was still normally passive at that time) for the cloister, it was her duty to marry, and who would want to marry a dowdy little frump? After marriage, though she should abandon youthful frivolities, she should not make life difficult for her husband by looking dreary. The same liberty to dress well was to be accorded to widows who intended to remarry, though those who did not so intend should dress more plainly, or they might mislead would-be suitors. This was a severely practical point of view, but it shows a considerable evolution in the attitude of Christians to married women. The fact that a girl intending to marry, and a married woman, were to adorn

themselves in order to please a potential or
actual husband shows that marriage was no
longer regarded as a distasteful duty for the
pious Christian. It was good and necessary that
a husband should take pleasure in his wife's
appearance, with the unstated consequence that
he would find it easier to remain faithful to an
attractive woman. This really means that it was
now considered legitimate, even laudable, for a
woman to be sexually attractive to her husband
on purpose.

The other tradition, which continued to
regard marriage as a degrading necessity pre-
cariously hallowed by the sacrament of matrimony, continued strong in spite of this. With it
went the assumption that personal adornment
was incompatible with true piety, and was, in
however small a degree, a concession to the
"world" (an essentially wicked place from which
sincere Christians were bound to withdraw
themselves). This attitude to marriage is well
exemplified in the ideas of the parents of St
Thérèse of Lisieux, who are, extraordinarily,
still held up as a model for Catholic families. To
both her parents marriage was a second-best, a
despairing alternative to the religious life they
had longed for. At the beginning of his married
life, Monsieur Martin intended that the union
should never be consummated, though later he
was persuaded to change his attitude, to the relief of his wife, who saw little point to a marriage
without children. One biographer, describing

the bedroom of the Martin couple at Alençon, refers to it as "sacred to the memory of a married love that ever sought to be nothing but a duty". This new unpopular view of Christian morality does probably reflect quite truly the feelings of the couple. Madame Martin later told her daughters that while good married couples might have "crowns of red roses" in heaven, the desirable "crowns of white roses" were reserved for the virgins. Zélie Martin was too good a Christian to think that marriage, being a state sealed by a sacrament, could be anything but good, but she undoubtedly felt that the physical side of marriage was an unpleasant necessity to be avoided if possible by her children. This not uncommon disgust at and suspicion of the body was reflected, as usual, in the family's attitude to dress. Though the children were well, even expensively, dressed, according to their middle-class social position, they were actively discouraged from taking pleasure in their appearance. Thérèse herself, as a very small child, longed to wear a frock with short sleeves for a party because she had pretty arms and knew that such a dress suited her. Her mother ordered that a long-sleeved dress be put on her. Thérèse sulked a little, privately, but grew to accept the idea herself.

This negative attitude to dress, and to anything that suggested an interest in the body, was taken for granted by most nineteenth-century Catholics. The more generous ideas of St Francis were for the time being either forgotten or interpreted in a sense that fitted in with the contemporary attitude of fear and hostility towards "the world", and its reprehensible habits. And this attitude persists. Although the Catholic understanding of the vocation of the laity, of the nature and value of Christian marriage (including sex in marriage) has developed enormously, the old attitude to personal adornment lingers on. This is true not only of the (decreasing) number of people who still feel that any attention to personal appearance is a concession to "the world". It is to be found, more insidiously, in the general assumption that such things as dress and make-up are a matter of indifference, provided due modesty is preserved. "There's no harm in it" is a fair summary of the attitude of most modern Christians to the feminine preoccupation with dress and kindred subjects. This word "indifferent" itself leads to misunderstanding. An act can be morally indifferent in itself, it cannot be morally indifferent when it is performed by a human being. The person who does it intends good, or intends ill, or at least suffers an effect of good or ill, however small the degree of either may be. We have been warned about this: "He that is not for me is against me." If Christians pass over as "indifferent" something which matters enormously in the lives of millions they are virtually handing over that particular aspect of the lives of those millions to the enemy for exploitation. And the field for exploitation is enormous, for one would have to be very simple-minded not to see that a woman's attitude to personal adornment is closely linked to her attitude to sex.

(If I discuss this as if it were entirely the concern of women it is partly because I am myself a woman, and therefore perhaps understand the feminine point of view, but also because it is held to be more tactful, in our society, to pretend that men have only a limited interest in their own appearance, and that for the most lofty motives only. In fact the motives are basically the same, and the veneer of indifference is visibly crumbling nowadays. But by preserving the fiction that women only are concerned in this matter it remains possible for male readers to wear the cap if it fits.)

It is difficult in discussing dress (and related subjects) not to get involved in a discussion of the psychology of sex. If I make strenuous efforts not to do so it is not because I underestimate the importance of the sexual significance of dress and other forms of adornment but because indirectly the larger subject would swamp the lesser one which is my present concern.

If it is accepted that personal adornment is a matter of importance, to women at least, and that no human act can be morally indifferent, it is clearly necessary to discover the Christian value of acts and states of mind connected with the decoration of the human body.

When some habit, job, activity, occasion, or

what have you, is normally considered in a non-Christian or even anti-Christian context, the attempt to put it in a Christian context is sometimes referred to as "Christianizing" it. This is a very misleading term, because it implies (and the implication is too often accepted by Christian and non-Christian alike) that to Christianize it means to wrench it out of its natural form in order to make it fit into a Christian pattern for which it was not designed. The opposite is the case. With actions, or whatever, that are not in themselves evil, but may be used for evil ends, the need is to discover their true "shape" and purpose, and re-form them according to the original design. If Christianity means anything at all it is the design for the perfection of the whole of human life. Everything in human nature that is good, even though the good may not at first be obvious, must find its fullest development in the Christian way of life. If we decide that some human activity or preoccupation cannot find its place in the Christian life then either the thing is fundamentally bad, or our ideas about Christianity are distorted or too narrow. If, therefore, we can honestly decide that there is nothing fundamentally corrupt about the urge to decorate the human body, it follows that an idea of Christian living that makes no provision for this appetite is in need of correction and widening.

As with all human appetites, there are occasions and vocations which demand that its normal satisfaction be denied. To fast does not imply a contempt for food, to embrace virginity does not (or should not) mean a refusal to recognize the goodness of sexual union in marriage. Many vocations, not only the "religious" vocation, demand the adoption of a way of dressing that is a symbol, to the individual and to others, of a special dedication. The nun does not wear a habit in order to look ugly but in order to show to herself and others that she has renounced the preoccupations of marriage or a career "in the world" in order to gain extra psychological freedom for the service of Christ in his brethren. (There are habits that make their wearers look ridiculous. This is usually an historical accident, will probably disappear soon, and certainly has nothing to do with the essential purpose of religious dress, which should symbolize not only a withdrawal from worldly concerns but also the dignity and beauty of the religious vocation.) Other men and women, not members of religious orders or even of secular institutes, may, for valid reasons, decide to adopt a simpler, more severely practical, way of dressing than their contemporaries. They may have a personal vocation (this applies to married couples as well) to a life that requires this extra detachment from the normal concerns of people "in the world". When this is a rational decision, and not a slightly smug assumption of superiority to a preoccupation that appears frivolous, it is good, positive and fruitful.

But I am chiefly concerned here with those whose vocation does not require them to renounce the pleasures—and problems—of personal adornment. To leave all this side of life in a limbo of Christian irrelevance is to leave it permanently open to misuse. In a life which is trying to be really Christian it sets up an artificial tension, because this part of life cannot then be brought into the life of prayer. It becomes a source of guilt and unease, and may gradually undermine the interior life which attempts to exclude it.

It is curious that anyone should still feel that a woman who takes pleasure in and trouble about her personal appearance is guilty of "vanity" even in the mildest degree. If it is right for her to look pretty—and she can't help it if God made her so—then it is only sensible that she should acknowledge the fact with due gratitude. There is an idea that while it is legitimate to look pretty if you are made that way it is wrong to try to enhance natural beauty, or to improve matters if you are not born beautiful. Yet nobody thinks it wrong to operate on a hare-lip or club foot. If surgery to repair a deformity is a good thing, why is it frivolous to improve the shape of your eyebrows, or powder a shiny nose? The moral objections to make-up and dress can be seen to be irrational because they usually draw quite arbitrary limits: powder is all right, false eye-lashes are suspect. A pretty cotton dress

is fine, more sophisticated fashions are
"worldly".

This is negative. It is not hard to show that
embellishment of natural endowment is sensible
and not wrong, but the matter goes much deeper
than that. The priest goes to the altar robed in
the best and most beautiful vestments that
parish funds can achieve and the parish taste
will permit. This is good and right because he
stands at the altar as the representative of Christ
and as the people's representative before the
throne of God. His adornment is a symbol of
our worship. The greatness of the work to be
done is worthy of the most beautiful garments
we can manage to provide. And surely it is not
only legitimate but right that the priest so
attired should take pleasure in the dignity and
beauty of his appearance because in it he is
better fitted to carry out his task. Better fitted
not only from the point of view of those who
see him, but from his own. This is very important. Any child who has taken part in a school
play knows the transformation that takes place
in the feeling of the actors when at last they are
allowed to rehearse in costume. Now they "feel"
their part, they act with a conviction and confidence that was lacking before. Clothes do effect
a real psychological, as well as external, change.
The priest vested for the altar is really different,
inside and out, from the pastor out on parish
calls. Properly understood, the vestments serve to

transform him interiorly, to develop and support his understanding of his vocation so that he may approach more nearly to the ideal that informs him.

If this be true of the priest, may we not extend the idea and consider whether the laity, who also have their part in the act of worship, may not be able to consider their outward appearance as an expression, and an aid to the development, of their vocation as Christians?

The woman who is married, or expects to be married, finds in that vocation her place in the worshipping community. When she comes to offer the sacrifice of the Eucharist she is offering her life as expressed in that vocation.

The vocation of marriage involves the need and duty to give pleasure to her husband, not only as an efficient cook and housekeeper, but also and chiefly as a lover. To please her husband sexually she will not, if she has any sense, despise the help of clothes and make-up as a general and particular preparation for love-making. It is unlikely that a man will get the maximum amount of pleasure from making love to a wife who has made no attempt to render herself desirable until she actually gets into bed. And as other women will frequently take the trouble to look attractive the dowdy wife is acting uncharitably in placing a quite unnecessary strain on her husband's affection, though the very young and the raving beauty can no doubt afford to be careless. It would not be reasonable to expect a hard-working mother and housewife always to look as if she had just left a beauty salon, and no sane husband would expect it, but there is a happy medium.

In passing, it is worth considering the matter of modesty. What is felt to be immodest at one period is acceptable at another. It is conceivable, though not likely, that complete nakedness might come to be generally accepted as perfectly compatible with modesty. The real need is to avoid a display of physical charm such as might hurt the conscience of another. It is possible to be violently immodest when dressed in a mackintosh and wellingtons. It is also possible, though difficult, to be modest in a bikini. But although a display of sexual charm to a man you are not married to and have no intention of marrying is wrong, "modesty" is entirely out of place between husband and wife. For a Christian young woman to wear blatantly seductive clothes in public would generally be wrong, but it is arguable that a wife would be virtuous and praise-worthy who (if she could afford them) wore extremely "daring" and seductive clothes for her husband's pleasure. Must the most "exciting" clothes be left for the use of those who abuse and degrade the sexual appetite? Must the suburban housewife find (or try not to find) compensation in erotic daydreams for the dullness of her real sex life? Perhaps the day will come when a Christian wife will give as much prayerful thought to the subject of looking seductive for her husband as another woman might give (barring the prayers) to her plans for attracting a new lover. If sex in marriage is good, and the pleasure it gives is intended by God, then anything that assists or enhances the pleasure is good too. And the increased pleasure must affect the whole relationship. The husband who knows that his wife cares enough for him to take the extra trouble to look as attractive as possible will respond to her affection with increased desire, certainly, but also with increased gratitude, respect and lasting devotion. Naturally, the expenditure of both time and money on dress and make-up must be governed by prudence and common sense. Incomes differ, and so do families, and with them the proportion of family income that should be given in alms. But when there is only so much money to spare it is not necessarily more prudent and Christian to spend it on new curtains rather than a new dress, on floor polish rather than nail varnish.

Just as the priest becomes better fitted for his task by the help of the vestments he wears for it, so a woman who wears clothes and make-up that "make the best of her" feels an increased confidence in her power to fulfil her vocation. It has been said that to be really well dressed a woman must be able to forget her clothes. This "forgetfulness" means that she is sure she looks her best, and, with the confidence and "lift" this gives her, she is free to devote all her energies to whatever demands are made on her. She does not "forget" her appearance in the sense that she does not care about it. If a woman can manage to feel confident of her own beauty and power to please she *will* please.

The Christian wife, then, goes to church in her capacity as a wife. She goes decked in her best clothes, not to show off, or because "everyone does", but because her contribution to the sacrifice of thanksgiving is derived from her success as a wife and mother. The clothes she wears in church will naturally be suited to the occasion, but they should be feminine and as beautiful as her income allows. They are the symbol of her vocation. Just as the differing vestments of the various sacred ministers make clear the fact that their functions differ, so the clothes of the congregation gathered to offer the Eucharistic prayer show the variety in unity of the People of God. Nurse, nun, soldier, those in distinctive uniforms are easy to pick out. A greater uniformity of dress among, paradoxically, non-uniformed callings, blurs many distinctions. But at least the Christian woman, wife, or potential wife, shows by her dress what is her part in the life of the Christian community. Whether her taste and income dictate pretty cottons or gaudy silks or a more sober elegance, she is proclaiming the fact that she worships God as a woman, that she is not ashamed of her femininity and all that that implies. She shows that it is by her feminine qualities, including her power of attracting the

opposite sex, that she is trying to fulfil her vocation, and so do her part in building the Kingdom of God on earth.

If all goes well the older woman gradually
finds a different use for her femininity. As a grand-
mother she has a part to play that is often mini-
mized, to the great loss of family life. She is free,
now that her children are grown-up, to be helper
and confidante to a wider circle of people, young
and old, than was formerly possible. Her experience and sympathy are at the service of many
who need it, in and outside her own family. The
love of husband and wife has deepened and
grown, and their dependence on each other has
achieved a unity and confidence that is a support to both in their efforts to serve others. Her
clothes reflect that change. She does not waste
time in a futile attempt to look young, but finds
pleasure in the dignity of richer colours and
textures, perhaps of jewellery that would once
have looked too heavy or gaudy.

The woman who, whether by choice or because "the right man" never turns up, remains
unmarried, does not thereby cease to be feminine. Unless she decides that her personal
vocation requires her to adopt a definitely "un-
worldly" style of dress she will, like her married
sisters, have to give some attention to what she
wears. The same principle, then, applies. Her
clothes show what she is, a woman in the world,
doing her best to use all her qualities in the
service of God.

It is an undoubted fact that non-Christians are repelled by the uniform of dowdiness too often adopted by the pious. If that is what Christians are like, they say to themselves, then I can do without Christianity. On the other hand, the Christian man or woman who is well dressed, confident, and obviously at ease in the world, without in any way compromising Christian principles, makes a real impression. It may be only a superficial impression, but the opportunity to deepen it is there.

But even if this apostolic justification were not present, could it be right for the Christian always to look less well groomed, less careful of her (or his) appearance, as if faith made the body a matter for shame? Christianity, in contrast to many other religions, emphasises the value and goodness of the human body. God himself took human flesh. Christians are the last who should think appearance of no importance. At the very least it might be considered that it is an act of charity to look nice. The presence of an attractively dressed woman can make the whole day seem brighter, and the companionship of a dowdy one can be depressing even to the most cheerful. This is at least partly due to the fact that the well dressed woman feels confident and happy, and the feeling is catching. The dowdy girl or woman often feels dreary, shy, and probably a little guilty, though whether the dowdiness is cause or effect it would be hard to say. Even the cheerful dowdy, who dresses badly from exuberant inattention rather than because of the more usual lack of confidence and fear of the public gaze, irritates by her carelessness though she is forgiven for the sake of her essential attractiveness as a person.

The relation between dress and state of mind is inescapable. Married, single, or widow, the Christian woman who dresses well, according to her means and way of life, faces life with confidence in her vocation as a woman and as a Christian. As such she is a witness for Christ. Her adornment celebrates her dignity as a woman and a Christian and expresses her joy and gratitude to God who made her.

If dressing is not only necessary but an important part of Christian living, it may be worth while to consider how it might be possible to make our understanding of its significance constant and deep. So many influences incline us to regard clothes and make-up as irrelevant to Christian life, and indeed as antagonistic to it. Advertisements try to attract us with a hint of forbidden fruit, by raising the desire for power, sexual or social, or for prestige. We need some specific means to make clear to ourselves our purpose as Christians. The priest vesting for Mass prays, as he puts on each garment, a prayer that recalls the symbolism of the garment and its use, and asks that he may use it fitly, and though the symbolism may be forced and the design of the garments in urgent need of reconsideration the principle is sound. In a busy life

getting up is always in a hurry, prayers are apt
to be skimped. But everyone has to get dressed,
and most women make up their faces as well.
It should be possible to ensure that some prayer
was offered if prayer and dressing could be combined. Workaday clothes suggest the prayer that
the work may be well done, in the service of
God. Party clothes suggest a prayer of thanksgiving, and one that their beauty may be used to
please but not to delude. It is a personal matter
in which individual needs, worries and desires
would suggest the right ideas. A woman making
up her face looks at it closely. She looks anxiously
for the first little lines, and might remember to
pray for grace to grow old peacefully, getting
the best from each stage of life, and knowing
that each year passed is a year nearer eternity.
The carefully made-up eyes warn her to pray for
grace to look at the world with the eyes that seek
what is good, love it and develop it. Lipstick reminds her to try to use speech to make, not
break, to build up, not to pull down. As she puts
on nail-varnish or just washes her hands she
thinks of all the things her hands do during the
day, and prays that she may do them well, and
for God, and that her mind may be gentle and
careful as her hands. The possibilities are endless, and adaptable to everyone. Similarly bath-
ing and going to bed at night takes on a new
significance. Taking off one's clothes is, or can
be, a sort of test of integrity, of how much of a
life is real and how much play-acting. If clothes

can express a vocation and help to develop it, they can also be a disguise. Getting undressed can be an examination of conscience, and an unwillingness to consider the fact of one's self unclothed is in itself a symptom of an evasion of reality.

All in all, it seems that personal adornment is far from being a frivolous subject unworthy of serious thought. How a person dresses is a clue to her deepest emotional secrets, including those of which she is not herself aware. Dress betrays what is beneath (in every sense). It can help to develop latent qualities, good or bad. What you put on your body shows what you think about yourself, and what you want to do with yourself. It is the symbol of vocation and a means to its fulfilment.

Apart from individual callings, the vocation of every Christian is to respond to the call of Christ by the total gift of body, mind and soul to his service. The Church is called the bride, but the Church is people, each one a complex of body and soul. Here on earth the right adornment of the body is a fitting symbol of the bridal adornment of the beloved for her lover, the Christian for Christ.

6

SEX, LAUGHTER (AND LAWRENCE)

IF they are honest with themselves (many aren't) the majority of younger adults will know that sex is the subject that preoccupies them most. Certain things—starvation, mental illness, overwhelming financial worry, or the drive of genius—may obliterate this. A true vocation may absorb and canalize it. But those who are not driven by genius or calling, are reasonably healthy and have enough to eat and live on, think about, talk about, worry about, or joke about sex during a large part of their waking lives. And when they sleep they even dream about it.

At a certain stage in life, that is, during adolescence and early grown-up life, this is not only inevitable but necessary and healthy. (If every child had a *perfect* background and up-bringing perhaps "worry" would be the wrong word. But this is so rare as to be practically non-existent.) Sexual worry does occur, and is a necessary stage in development, as things are. It is essential to a well-balanced adulthood to understand, accept and learn to use (in the widest sense) the sexual powers. But after a certain period the worrying about sex should, ideally, be no longer necessary in principle, though sexual problems will almost certainly occur at various stages of life and need to be thought out and dealt with. If the foundation of a sane approach to sex has been laid in early life this should not involve worry so much as serious thought. Of course this is not always true—sexual problems are not so simple. But a good start should at least reduce the tensions, muddles and unnecessary suffering that result from trying to make inevitable sexual adjustments with inadequate mental and emotional equipment.

But even if the element of worry (and therefore possibly the dreams) should disappear after a while, the need to think about sex, and on occasion to talk about it with the right person, continues. It is part of being grown-up. Our understanding of sex—in its true and widest sense of the driving force of human nature—develops and grows with the whole personality.

So far so good. But there remains one element in this range of mental states with regard to sex that is not so easy to fit into the pattern of development. Thoughts, words, worries, dreams—what about the jokes?

Why do people make jokes about sex? Is this a good thing or a bad thing?

A glance into any bookshop or newsagent will be enough to show that these questions matter. Being funny about sex is an extremely lucrative business. As for spoken jokes, there are almost certainly more sex jokes than any other kind, if

you include those that turn on sex even if they
don't refer to it directly—those about henpecked
husbands, mothers-in-law, and similar subjects.

The short and usual answer given by Catholics
is that people joke about sex because they have
nasty minds, and that it is altogether a bad
thing.

Perhaps the whole subject needs to be examined a little more closely.

There is a common feeling among serious
people that it is wrong to joke about things that
matter. There is no doubt at all that sex matters,
and if this feeling is based on something true,
then certainly we shouldn't jest about sex. But
is it a true feeling?

What are jokes for? To make us laugh. But
why do we want to laugh? Laughter releases tension. During the War never a BBC "funny show"
passed without one or more jokes about the
Nazis. Did we find the real Nazis funny? Of
course not. As we crawled, year after year, under
the burden of conscious or subconscious fear of
them it was a relief to laugh at them. Nowadays
we make jokes about nuclear bombs. People
roared with slightly hysterical laughter at the
"nuclear" song of Tom Lehrer. It made us feel
better about the appalling threat that hangs
over us. Why? Two elements can perhaps be
discerned. Jokes always have an element of incongruity—the juxtaposition of something inescapably serious or fearful and something
essentially unimportant, harmless or trivial.

This brings the serious or frightening thing within our reach, as it were, and makes it therefore less frightening or less preoccupying. In the case of jokes about what frightens us we laugh for two different but complementary reasons: both because the tension is released, and because we feel we are somehow hitting back at the thing that frightens us, against which we are, otherwise, powerless. (It is noticeable that we do not laugh at things we are able to tackle in other ways.)

These two different kinds of laughter are often reactions to the same joke, but they are not alike. The laughter of release is innocent and good. It helps us to cope with emotions that might otherwise be unbearable. It helps us keep a sense of proportion. We see that where human beings are concerned even the most serious matters have their lighter, ludicrous side. (Animals and inanimate things are never ludicrous, unless we attribute to them human characteristics that do not belong to them.) This kind of laughter does not show any lack of respect for the seriousness of a serious subject. It is simply a kind of compensation for the limitations of our mental and emotional equipment, which are normally inadequate to deal with the really great matters "straight"—at least for any length of time— without danger of overstrain.

The other kind of laughter is malicious and destructive. It is our revenge for our impotence. It does no good, but rather degrades us. It does not relieve us or help us to face up to things, it leaves us feeling angrier and more helpless than before.

It seems probable that this need for revenge is the reason behind most sex jokes. People are driven by sexual needs and worries and find themselves powerless in the face of them. The only means of retaliation is by ridicule. By making this interior tyrant seem ridiculous, unworthy of any respect, the feeling is created (for a while) that one is the master. Sex is not my boss, I can do what I like with it, kick it about, hold it up to scorn; this is what is at the back of a certain, familiar, type of joke. But every thrust of malice and ridicule recoils, inevitably, on the attacker. It is himself that the joker attacks. One cannot divorce sex and self—though the idea (mostly implicit) that one can is a common enough refuge from responsibility. Whoever ridicules sex in this way is undermining his own personal value, making it, each time, more and more difficult to bring his sexuality into a balanced relationship with the rest of life. And the condition perpetuates itself, growing always worse —the ridicule makes sex seem always more unworthy and degrading, and yet this degrading thing continues to make its demands. Kick it, then. Get your own back. And cover up the process by telling yourself—and others—that it is normal, natural, only human, a bit of fun.

And yet the sexual act is, and remains, good. It has an essential goodness that nothing can

spoil. It contains within itself the seed of possible
redemption even from this process of tail-chasing
disgust. As a seed will absorb any nourishment
available, and grow, so this divine seed absorbs
into itself any remnant of good there is, even in
an apparently degraded human nature, and so
grows.

But what is it that makes the difference?
What, on the one hand, drives human nature to
attack its own sexuality as the source of its
degradation, and what, on the other, can make
that same sexuality the instrument of its salvation? Surely, pride on the one hand and humility
on the other.

Pride rejects something that seems to undermine human dignity. True sexual love means
giving, means sacrifice, means forgetfulness of
self. Pride will not give, and tries therefore to
regard the act as purely physical, an appetite to
be satisfied, leaving out of account as far as possible the needs of the partner. But that is not all.
The thing that pride will not accept, cannot
accept and live, is that there are aspects of sex
that are humiliating, even ludicrous.

And this is where the other, the innocent,
kind of laughter becomes relevant. Sex is good,
sex is of fundamental importance in human life,
sex is holy, God-created, God-bearing. All right—
but does all this apply to every aspect of sexual
activity? We are not in paradise. If we can really
approach the question honestly we must know
that the answer is, No. It is not enough to say,

sex is good, God made it. We have to remember that sex operates in human beings, in bodies and minds, both imperfect, both out of touch with their Creator, and with each other, muddled, not in full control, frightened and adrift.

It is good to realize that sex is holy, and we have to hang on to this, but this does not mean that we must therefore treat every aspect of sex with the same degree of reverence.

When one realizes this one comes slap up against Lawrence. Lawrence takes us by the lapel, and preaches the goodness and holiness of sex until our heads spin with his marvellous language and his conviction. To the shame of Christians be it said that this man who knew nothing of the reality of Christianity proclaimed the goodness of God's creation while Christians cleared their throats and made shocked noises. Of course it was the lack of the completeness that a Christian consciousness might have given him (if he had ever met a Christian capable of giving him even the vaguest clue to what the faith he thought he hated was really all about) that is the root cause of the unreality, the unhumanness, that flaws so much of Lawrence's work. But, fascinating as that subject is, it is with one single failure of understanding in Lawrence that I am concerned here.

With the zeal of a fanatic Lawrence preached the holiness of sex, and like all fanatics he made no distinctions about the object of his worship. He reminds one of those Catholic apologists who

4

rush to the defence of the indefensible and resent a criticism of aspects of peasant piety as
fiercely as they would a doubt cast on the divinity
of Christ. The result is that when Lawrence is
at his most deadly serious many even of his
admirers are seized with a desire to laugh. The
most glaring example, of course, is the much
debated *Lady Chatterley*. It is a tract, and has
the faults of most tracts. When the characters are
not being used to point the moral they fade into
nonentity. Lawrence isn't interested in them
except at the moments when they exemplify his
thesis. Neither, then, are his readers. (Connie is
one of the silliest young women ever to be
honoured by great writing.) So in this book no
"engagement" of the reader hides from him the
fact that in praising the unique goodness of
sexual love Lawrence is trying to force us to
admit that all the aspects of sex are of equal
virtue. And the result of this is, among all that
wonderful writing, passages of really dreadful
silliness. He cannot (or perhaps will not) see
that, because human nature is not perfect,
neither is its use of sex; that certain things about
it are *funny*. Funny because incongruous—funny
because of the inescapable proximity of the
beautiful and the ugly, the spiritual and the
grossly material, the sublime and the ridiculous.

This does not mean that there is anything that
is essentially ignoble about even the most purely
physical details of sex. But in the existing state
of human nature that is how they are felt. We

find forcibly confronted in sexual love the elements of the perennial conflict between "nature"
and the spirit.

Here, in this universal experience, the great
struggle that has preoccupied men through the
ages is found in its plainest and most obvious
terms. In the face of this challenging fact several
reactions are possible. One can pretend that no
such confrontation has taken place, that flesh
and spirit do not meet here but only flesh and
flesh. This is an ancient and ever popular heresy,
since the exalted soul is not held responsible for
the animal body. One may regard the whole
thing as spiritual, with the flesh as a vehicle
merely, and scarcely to be regarded. (Aldous
Huxley has something to say about this in relation to Shelley!) Or one may decide that the
spiritual does not exist, that the satisfaction of
the flesh is all that can be expected, and that
therefore no conflict exists except in diseased
minds. This is the view popularized so per-
suasively by Dr Alex Comfort in his book *Sex
in Society*, a work that Christians should read.
Lawrence's version is a subtle and impressive
variant of this. To him, the satisfaction of the
flesh is sufficient, but he sees it as summing up
and bringing into play all that is most marvellous
in human nature, so that anything that would
prevent it is evil. The conflict is that of the
essential goodness of human nature, perfectly
expressed in sexual love, with extraneous circumstances, even when their effects are interior.

Or one can struggle to be realistic. One can acknowledge fully the beauty of God's plan and yet not ignore the limitations that our physical nature imposes on it. One can look, and see that the most potentially perfect of human relationships must be expressed through the medium of bodies and minds whose workings we scarcely understand, even now, and which let us down at every turn.

Pride refuses such a lowering of dignity. But surely a Christian humility accepts it, and may express that acceptance by laughing. Such laughter does not insult the nobility of God's plan but temporarily resolves the tension we may feel when we see what the plan is and how it works out in practice. There is no laughter in heaven, said Mark Twain. True, because there is no incongruity in heaven. There, the perfect plan is seen in its perfection. Here, the plan may be perfect, but in the nature of things it cannot function perfectly. If we are realistic we know this. If we are humble we put up with it. If we are Christians we can embrace it, and laugh. And if we laugh, this kind of laughter is good, and healing, it breeds courage and kindness and charity. It is not the laughter of revenge, shaking impotent fists at God who imprisoned us in flesh. It is rather the laughter of children, who, not being burdened with final responsibility, can afford to be humble, and accept the incongruity of God in man.

7

THE CHRISTIAN HOME AND THE AFFLUENT SOCIETY

THERE is nothing intrinsically virtuous about scrubbing a stone floor, or about peeling potatoes, or about doing large quantities of washing by hand. It is not sinful to put down a good plastic floor covering and wipe it over easily with a damp cloth. Using a potato peeler is not one of the seven deadly sins, and the washing machine was not invented by the devil.

It would not be necessary to utter such obvious truths if it were not for a lingering puritanism in certain Christian circles that feels that a great deal of manual labour is not only beneficial to the soul, especially the female soul, but that to make use of the products of the industrial system is in some way to bow down to the idols of materialism.

Hard manual labour can be good; it is a tried and effective remedy against pride and sloth, an excellent penance, and can be an act of worship. But it is not an absolute good. It is not essential to human beings but only a necessity imposed by the imperfection of the human condition as we know it. It also brings with it a sense of achievement and satisfaction in the result which goes far to compensate for fatigue and unpleasantness.

In communities where industrialization does not exist or is only just beginning all the work of the home is done by hand. In that case the women (and it is mainly women who are concerned in the subject of this essay) make their lives round the routine of manual work, and, if they are Christians, seek their perfection in it. But it must be remembered that such communities, while they lack the advantages of more advanced societies, are also free of their problems. Less happy are those women who, because of individual or local economic hardship, must struggle to rear a family in a highly industrialized and generally prosperous society when they themselves must do without the aids that such a society provides for itself. Such families need an especial heroism, but it is not my purpose here to discuss the way of perfection for women in backward countries or in primitive areas of civilized countries, or for women who suffer individual hardship in an otherwise comfortable society. It is rather to discuss the best way of making use of what is good in the civilization of our age and country. The role of Christian parents in the home must remain broadly the same in every age and country, in the sense that the aim is always the same: that of bringing up children to serve God as well as possible. But the ways of compassing this end must vary widely.

In a predominantly Christian community, one which pays at least lip-service to Christian standards, the approach to the education of children must be different from that demanded of Christian mothers and fathers in a pagan or at least de-Christianized society. In our country the problem is complicated for Catholics by an inherited "ghetto" mentality. The outlook of many Catholics is that of civilians inside a besieged fortress. They intend to survive, with the hope that somehow outside help will make it possible for them to emerge and settle down outside the walls, but they do not expect or intend to make any move themselves to remedy their enclosed condition. This attitude, understandable a hundred years ago, is ludicrous today. Catholics are constantly being exhorted to take their proper place in public life, to try to influence society in their various professions and trades. The response is not encouraging, though of course there are many individuals who do their best to make up for the apathetic mass. This is partly the fault of Catholic schools— from primary to public—where, with few exceptions, the aim is to turn out "good practising Catholics", and the religious instruction is based mainly on the idea of defending the Faith against attack, mainly a type of attack which is now practically non-existent.

But if the schools are to blame it is to be

remembered that parents get the schools they deserve. If parents supinely hand over to the schools the responsibility for educating their children as Christians they cannot complain of the result. If the Christian community as a whole demanded a more vital approach to the teaching of the Faith it would be forthcoming and I have discussed this in more detail in another essay. But it is unlikely that out-of-date ideas and methods will change when each new generation of teachers comes from homes which feel no obligation to think about the Faith themselves and certainly never question the ways in which it is taught in the schools. Teachers are not a race apart. They get their ideas from their parents and later from their training colleges where they are taught by teachers themselves reared in an unchanged tradition. The chance of change is even less likely when the teachers are from a religious order. These will often be people who found the atmosphere and traditions of their own schooldays congenial. They responded to the good in them and found their vocation in carrying on the system. But with the good they also carry on things that are out of date. Without stimulation or demand from outside how can parents expect them to realize that there is something wrong? If Christian education is to be improved parents have the greater responsibility for initiating changes. The primary responsibility for the education of Christian children lies on their parents and the parish priest. When these work together, and help to make the needs of the children clear, some teachers at least will respond with enthusiasm, and their example will gradually spread new ideas.

If the first responsibility rests on parents, it is necessary for them to face the facts of daily life in contemporary Western society. Whether or not we regard it as a good way of life, this is the way it is. Politically, we may try to alter it, but domestically we have to find out what is good in it, and then make the best possible use of that good, in the task of educating our children as Christians.

Since it is the mothers who spend most time with the children it is they who have to deal with most of the problems and challenges of this task. The father's help and support are indispensable, but it is the mother who will put into practice the ideas and methods they work out together. Therefore it is from the mother's point of view that I want to look at this subject of Christian education in the affluent society.

There are two quite different factors that have radically affected the way mothers are able to carry out their vocation here and now. One is the obvious fact that labour-saving gadgets and better planned houses can, when intelligently used, give a wife and mother more leisure than was previously imaginable except for those who were lucky enough to have several servants. The other is the great improvement in the education of women.

These two things are complementary in the vocation of a Christian mother. The gadgets, carefully chosen to meet individual needs and used in such a way as to get the maximum benefit from them in time and effort saved, are important tools of her trade to a woman who wants to bring up a Christian family in the modern world. In any group of mothers talking it is usually the case that the admiration goes to the one who performs the greatest amount of physical labour: the one who makes all the family's clothes, for instance, who bottles umpteen jars of fruit. And most women do feel a curious kind of shame when they admit that they buy their children's clothes, and don't bottle any fruit; this, in spite of the fact that ready-made clothes are sometimes cheaper than, and can be just as good as, home-made ones and that, unless you have a large productive garden, bottling fruit saves little. It is not a waste of time to do these things; they can be very satisfying as well as useful. They give pleasure to the good housewife and her family feel a pride in her achievements, but it is desirable that a mother should use her brains to decide how much or how little of her time she can reasonably give to such occupations in relation to her other responsibilities at any given period in her family's growth. She should not allow herself to be swayed by the prestige attached to domestic arts and crafts in women's magazines and organizations, admirable as some of these are. There are of course many cases in which every other consideration has to give way to the need for living on a very small wage or pension. I am not considering these at the moment because I am discussing opportunities in the kind of society we are aiming at, though we have only partly achieved it—one in which a fairly high standard of living is the norm, and comparative financial security the rule. It is, in any case, the responsibility of mothers who do enjoy a fair measure of material wellbeing to bring up children who will help those who do not.

The use of labour-saving gadgets and ready-made clothes is, after all, a negative matter. Intelligent use of these things is necessary to give women the time they need for other more important things. If, for one reason or another, a busy mother has to do without them, she can count on the Holy Spirit to help her to manage somehow, but that does not mean that endless heavy physical labour is either necessary or desirable for a mother. A natural and right admiration for the heroism of women who struggled to bring up their children as Christians in spite of a burden of poverty and never-ending work sometimes misleads preachers and writers into confusing their difficulties with their virtues. Because good women in the past had a lot of heavy work to do and managed to bring up their children as excellent Christians, therefore heavy physical work is regarded as necessary for anyone who wishes to bring up children as good Christians. The fallacy is obvious, but the conclusion is still proclaimed with fervour and conviction. It would be truer to say that neither heavy work nor the lack of it in itself helps a mother to follow her vocation, but that less fatigue and more time do at least give her more opportunities to make use of the other major asset of the modern woman—her better education. She may make an excellent job of rearing her family in spite of constant fatigue and lack of time. But such conditions are, in themselves, bad, not good, just as illness or poverty may be sanctified but that does not make it good.

Leisure, then, is a good thing for a Christian mother to have, and a good education should help her to make intelligent use of it. I do not mean that all modern girls are well educated. They aren't: Catholic girls, in particular, often receive a very cramped and negative kind of training, surrounded by warnings and cautions. If those who struggle to give their pupils a sane and well balanced education resent this suggestion I need only quote one case out of many: a Catholic girl who, about to be married, believed that sexual intercourse in marriage was a mortal sin. She was the product of an esteemed convent school. But they can get at least the rudiments of an understanding of the history of their country and its literature, they have the opportunity to learn to think and to take an interest in politics and welfare if they want to.

It might be worth considering something that at first sight appears to be a peculiar reversal: that it may be easier for a wife than for a husband to keep up an interest in current affairs, including current Church affairs. The very fact that the mother of a young family does not get out into the world of factory or business or profession gives her the chance to take a wider view of many questions on which her husband's ideas may be influenced by the conditions of his particular job or the opinions of those he works with. I do not think I am simply suggesting a new occasion for marital discord. I am quite serious in thinking that it is part of the job of a wife and a mother to be a well informed citizen, both of her own country and of the world. This is generally taken for granted in the case of "career girls" and professional women, but it is assumed that because a home and young children keep a woman from direct participation in, say, local politics or organized Christian Action it is no longer necessary for her to have any ideas on subjects outside the domestic round. But how are mothers to bring up their children to take an intelligent interest in the life of the Church and of their country if they themselves are passive and uninterested? During the greater part of childhood and adolescence the children's father will be at best only an occasional companion. The stimulus of his interests and

opinions is very important, but lack of time and
the need to concentrate on getting a livelihood
limit his influence in the earlier years—the
years that matter. For it is in the years up to
adolescence that the habits of mind and body
are formed. And it is during those years that
children have to be encouraged to think for
themselves, constantly to question, to explore, to
discover both with their hands and their minds.

It is so easy to kill curiosity. Some schools are
expert at it. Any tendency to pursue a line of
enquiry beyond the strict limits of the lesson
in progress is too often regarded as a serious
scholastic sin. Children who come to school full
of eagerness and alert curiosity become, in a
matter of months, accustomed to the idea that
lessons are a necessary bore and knowledge something imposed by grown-ups. And it can be the
same at home: so often the answer to children's
questions is "I don't know, dear", in a tone that
implies that there is no need for anyone to know.
Even more common is: "Do be quiet! Can't you
see I'm busy?" And after a while the child stops
asking questions. And when later he needs to
ask important personal questions, he doesn't.
Mother isn't a person who has ideas about anything. But she should have. She should have the
time and the will to have ideas, to read and to
think.

Yet even if the modern home can give her the
time she needs, the will is often lacking. It is
often much more difficult to do a bit of serious

reading than to make jam, and the chances are that friends and neighbours will regard the reading as waste of time—if not a form of showing off—while the jam-maker is admired. But a lot of women would make the necessary effort if they realized how important it is, and how rewarding. The mother who takes the time and trouble to answer her children's questions has the satisfaction of watching their minds reach out to new ideas as they follow up the interesting subject. If she doesn't know the answer at once—and one often does not—then mother and children can find it out together, by looking it up in an encyclopedia, or by a visit to a museum or public library. Of course, children always want to know at once, and in this case it is worth while to do what they want. Does it really matter if we have a snack lunch for once in order to get out earlier? Is it really so important to get all the ironing finished? It is, like so many minor domestic decisions, a question of priorities. Of course the household chores have to be done, but it is very easy to get into the habit of making the children fit in with the chores instead of arranging the routine so as to give the children the time they need. A busy housewife and mother has to be very clear in her mind about which things matter most or her daily struggle to keep the house or flat and the children reasonably clean and tidy and the family well fed will little by little absorb all her energies. Then long-ago plans and enthusiasm about

reading to and with the children, about teaching
them songs or encouraging hobbies and interests,
are gradually forgotten. The physical welfare of
the family becomes an end in itself and even
the children for whose sakes she works so hard
appear to her as obstacles to her labours. It is
this state of mind that often makes women snap
and natter at their children, and shoo them out
to find their amusements as best they can. Then
the undesirable nature of their chosen pursuits
and companions rouses her to further complaints
and reproaches. If she ever notices that other
children seem to be developing better, or have
wider interests, or greater family affection, this
only irritates her, and she blames the children
rather than herself. So it goes on until in the
end they leave home, resentful, unsatisfied and
uneducated, for ever handicapped by a distorted
education and an inability to develop proper
human relationships. Yet such a mother can tell
herself, and her neighbours, that she has "always
done her best for them", and perhaps she really
believes it. But she hasn't. She says she had no
time to do more, but this only means that she
put last things first and spent on domestic chores
(perhaps beautifully and meticulously performed) time that belonged by right to the children. There are, of course, all too many women
who are so tired and overworked that they could
not, if they wanted to, help their children to
develop their interests in any way but by an
assurance of their affection. (This is in itself a

great deal.) But the woman who needs to stop and question herself, not once but regularly, on the use to which she puts her time is the mother who finds herself saying, "Can't you see I'm busy?", or "Do go and play", every time (not just some of the times) her children make demands on her attention. If her examination of conscience tells her that she is exalting her household duties at the expense of her children's development then it is time to reorganize. Our children have minds as well as bodies. A mother who serves only their bodies is bringing up a family of stunted human beings.

The pursuit of information is not the only way in which children need their mother's help and time. It is not only intellectual interests—scientific, historical or what-have-you—that need to be stimulated in order to develop a complete human being. Most mothers spend a large part of their time preventing, or clearing up, various kinds of "mess". If they used a quarter of this time in helping the children to make really interesting messes, the gain to the whole family would be enormous. Children need to use their hands and eyes as well as their minds. Reading a book is a tidier occupation than keeping snails or making clay pots, but a purely intellectual education is only half an education. The exploration of things with hand and eye not only satisfies the mind, it stimulates it. We all get a bit sick of the word "creative" as used by educationists. It can too easily be used by the incompetent teacher or parent to cover an unwillingness to tackle difficult mental disciplines. But it really does matter that a child should be allowed and helped to make things, and to make them well. Clay-modelling, painting, pressing flowers, making baskets, carpentry, chemical experiments, keeping animals, making a museum, sewing, acting, they all make more or less of a mess. No housewife objects to the mess on the kitchen table when she is making pastry, or to the snips of material scattered on the floor when she is dress-making. But if children put paint on the table or wood shavings on the floor she easily feels annoyed, because these things are only "play" and therefore not necessary. The same applies to unmessy but noisy pursuits like singing or home-made percussion bands. We want to block our ears and say, "Do be quiet!" Their play must not interfere with our convenience. But the divine wisdom is described as "playing in the world", and if our children are to grow in that wisdom they must play that kind of play— the play of making things. If the things they make and do can also be used directly in the learning of their faith, so much the better. They can model their own crib figures and dress them, make their own Madonna for their bedrooms, paint or model the Stations of the Cross, fetch flowers for our Lady's altar, and act Christmas plays or make "music" for them. All these things can help them to learn their faith and to love it with hands and feet and ears and eyes as well as with their minds. But all their making and doing is religious, even if it is not directed to specifically religious ends. It is all part of their education as the complete human beings that God wants them to be.

There is nothing specially modern about children's need to "make a mess". What is new —and bad—is the tendency to substitute ready-made entertainments for self-made ones that require, initially, more effort, more mess and perhaps more room. I am not condemning television. It can play a fascinating and stimulating part in the education of children. But like all tools it needs to be used with intelligence and purpose, not just because it's there. This is a case where we have to revive what was once taken for granted rather than to work out something new. Catering for the need of our children to make and explore and discover can be difficult in modern cramped conditions but no amount of purely intellectual stimulus can be a substitute for it.

In a civilization in which, for good or ill, more and more of the things we need are going to be produced by automatically operated machines, surely it makes sense to suggest that our children, when they grow up, will want to make beautiful and useful things, not because they must, as in the days of cottage industries, but just for the love of making? Then they will be able to use and love in their homes the things they have had time to make because the machines have done for them what was dull but necessary. In a society that aims at constantly increasing its leisure this seems to be a possible answer to the fears of those who see in industrialization a threat to man's need to create. Efficient industrialization should, on the contrary, provide the leisure in which the need to create can be given full play. We should be able to work at making lovely things—music or jugs or pictures or gardens or chairs—for our own enjoyment and that of our friends and neighbours. William Morris might have rejoiced if he could have seen what the machines he hated might one day do to liberate human beings from repetitive and meaningless tasks and give them time to make. But if *News from Nowhere* ever becomes news from here it will be because a new generation of children has learnt to love making, and they will not do this if they never have a chance to "make a mess". Even the school craft classes cannot make up for lack of encouragement at home. The scorn poured on "all that nonsense" that does not help in passing the all-important exams can kill a child's awakening interest stone dead. Once again, the real responsibility rests on the parents.

So the time saved by a sensible use of gadgets and by the non-scrubbing of floors is to be used, first, to educate one's children. All knowledge is worth having, and wide interests are necessary in the mother to stimulate wide interests in the children. If she is an alert, adventurous, experimenting person, she will bring up children with the same qualities.

But for us who are Christians there is one kind of knowledge which is of capital importance because it provides, or should provide, the framework into which all the rest is fitted. Teaching the children their religion is of course a perennial part of a mother's work, but there are special difficulties confronting us, here and now, in Western society in the sixties, because of the kind of society into which our children will emerge. Personal goodness and piety are, as always, enormously important, and there is no need to enlarge on that because there is nothing especially modern in the need for holiness in the mother of Christian children. But it isn't enough. There are women of undoubted personal holiness, who compel admiration by their unfailing cheerfulness under difficulties, their charity and courage; yet when the children whom they have carefully trained grow up they begin to doubt the religion they have been taught. Without losing their love and respect for the mother who taught them they gradually abandon—partly at least—the beliefs and moral standards in which she trained them. What was lacking? I think what they missed was an element of intellectual toughness underneath the piety. They were told things, but not directly encouraged to question; they were instructed, but not stimulated. In fact they were not used to thinking about their religion.

This, then, is a field in which it must be a moral duty for a mother to be well informed. The need for honest reappraisal discussed in the first essay, which affects all Christians, has a particular practical force in the case of a mother or anyone concerned with teaching children. She needs to know more than the Catechism answers. She needs to read about, for instance, recent developments in scriptural studies, about the liturgical revival and what it means. How many intelligent adolescents have begun their drift away from the Faith because they thought they were obliged to believe in the literal truth of some Old-Testament myth? To read one of the many books for laypeople on the study of Scripture by perfectly orthodox writers can be an eye-opener and an enormous relief to faithful but ill-instructed Catholics who had secretly been worried by Joshua's sun or Jonah's whale. It is for modern Christian mothers to see that their children do not regard the "miraculous" flight of the Holy House to Loreto as an article of the Creed, or the clumsy reporting of young visionaries as exact records of the opinions of the Mother of God. If we are to bring up well informed Christian citizens, they must be well informed Christians as well as well informed citizens. A faith that is clogged with half-buried doubts cannot give (even if faith survives) the impetus needed for a full Christian life in the modern world.

Naturally, no one woman can work up an

absorbing interest in every aspect of the history, life and teaching of the Church. But to have some idea of what is going on, and of the history behind modern developments, is not a luxury for the odd pious blue-stocking, but a necessity for every mother who wants to do her work efficiently. At present there is all too much truth in the popular impression that Catholic mothers are miserable, dowdy, over-worked drudges, with no ideas in their heads beyond the babies' nappies and their rosaries.

Of course not many are really like this; but the trouble is that a slightly sanctified version of this is offered to us as an ideal. The image of the meek, simple, devout mother who mutters Hail Marys over the washtub and is too absorbed in her children and her prayers to bother about her appearance is held up for our admiration and imitation. There is a very real kind of holiness that lies behind this subtly distorted image. The real thing, when one meets it, is admirable and deeply impressive. But this version of the ideal Catholic mother can too easily be an easy way out for people who don't want to face up to the demands of modern society as it affects the rearing of Christian children. Not only do some women find this distorted ideal a convenient excuse for mental laziness, but some clerics with more enthusiasm than clearsightedness have been known to encourage Catholic women to absolve themselves from the need for coming to grips with modern life.

The woman who has really faced up to the needs of her own family in the modern world will quite possibly be anxious to work for the satisfaction of those needs outside as well as inside her home. She will want to take her full share in the life of the parish, in local politics, in Christian action generally. In fact, to the more conservative, she may seem a menace, a woman who has forsaken her home and her children in order to interfere in affairs that have long been the province of the male—in particular the clerical male. Remembering that terrible race of unoccupied women who do spend their lives on committees, endlessly organizing other people, it is not surprising that the image of the docile, dowdy mother-at-home has its appeal. But the fact remains that a woman may be not forsaking but promoting her children's welfare by joining in outside activities once the children are old enough to do without her from time to time. If the laity—including the female laity— are really to play their full part in the Church then laypeople must be given the opportunity for action, and that means the opportunity for wrong or annoying action. To promote as an ideal a state of life that was forced on women of past generations by necessity is to contradict the whole of this new understanding of the role of the laity.

Our society needs mothers who are willing to tackle the complex business of bringing up children with intelligence and adaptability. More leisure and better education give us the opportunities we need; it is for us to make use of them and not to be put off by the unbalanced values, inside and outside the Church, of those who exalt physical labour and achievement at the expense of intellectual effort. In the last resort our children's souls are more important than pots of jam.

And when the children have grown up and gone away, what then? The woman who has dropped all interests but domestic ones faces a rather dreary future unless she is strong-minded enough to try to develop interests and skills that come comparatively easily in youth but are much more difficult to acquire in middle age. The woman who, for the sake of her children, has continued, or even perhaps begun, to learn to think and experiment, has every chance of making a full and useful life for herself. She will be less tempted than most to cling disastrously to her departing brood. And they will be glad to see her in their own homes because she will be an interesting and a stimulating person to have around.

There are terrible crises of conscience that can arise when Christians live in a prosperous society with a high standard of living. It was not for nothing that Christ constantly stressed the danger of preoccupation with money, and what money can buy. The proper use of wealth is the subject of another essay, for in the vocation of the modern woman at home it is a subject she has to face.

Holiness is attainable under any conditions, in any time or place, by making use of those conditions. Unless the surroundings in which the Christian finds himself are clearly and inescapably an occasion of sin, then it is his duty to turn them to good account as far as possible, and to use this good to help correct what is bad, as far as he is able. For good or ill we live in an "affluent" industrial society. Instead of moaning about the vices of our time let us set about using its virtues in the service of God.

8

POSSESSION AND POVERTY

PEOPLE who grew up during the last war, or who were at least fairly young at the time, may remember one considerable compensation for the shortages and difficulties of civilian life. This was the release from many of the problems of possessions and the desire for them. When there was very little of anything we were delighted with the little bits that came our way. The "find" in a junk shop; the "good prewar" dress that could be remade; the ecstatic discovery that theatrical suppliers were still allowed to dye their stuffs in brilliant colours when all the rest of the world was wearing drab; the unexpected food parcel; the party where the host or hostess did not feel obliged to hunt for a "gimmick", because it was so nice to have a party at all—all such little bits of pleasure had a special purity of motive because circumstances robbed us of most of the necessary equipment for showing-off, status-seeking, snobbery, one-upmanship. People envied each other their tins of corned beef or their snippet of prewar velvet, but even then it was part of a game; next time *we* might be lucky and acquire a tin of red paint or some coloured cups and saucers. Now, when pre-

Christmas shops are crammed with dazzling
baubles and ropes of tinsel, I remember with
nostalgia those wartime Christmas trees,
decorated with such ingenuity from all kinds of
unlikely scraps and oddments. They would look
shabby beside the brilliantly decked trees of the
sixties.

When people look back wistfully to the
anxious, threatened life of wartime England it is
not the hardships they miss, it is the blessed
simplicity of a life from which so many causes
of worry and tension had been forcibly removed.
Even an enforced poverty brought a little of the
lightheartedness, in spite of danger and un-
certainty, that is the prerogative of those un-
burdened by carefulness for possessions. There
was no temptation to buy furniture one could
not afford in order to keep up with the neighbours, for there was no furniture to afford. If
one's clothes were shabby, so were everyone else's.
If one had no car, neither had the Joneses. And
nobody had holidays abroad.

Poverty by itself does not bring release from
the itch of envy. People who, in a prosperous
society, have small incomes are far from immune
to the stings of acquisitiveness. Their envy may
be impotent but it is none the less irritant.

Can we hope for no remedy but the possibility
of a general lowering of the standard of living of
Western society? Are Christians so feeble that
they can see no cure for envy but the forcible
removal of temptation? Christians are too often

to be heard and read bewailing the modern greed for status, for possessions, for something—anything—more than the next family.

It is right to regard this as a bad thing, but wrong to see it as, in most cases, a sin, that is a deliberate wrong on the part of the individual.

It is a commonplace of advice given to parents by child psychologists that the child who grabs, who is unusually possessive about material objects, is a child who lacks a sense of security. Lacking it, perhaps through no-one's fault but because of some experience he cannot even remember, he tries to surround himself with visible, tangible possessions, as a substitute, artificial, form of security against a hostile world. This is a common cause of pilfering among school-children and of rivalry at home. One of its manifestations is in the child who cannot go to bed without his fetish—be it a teddy bear or a piece of old blanket—which protects him against harmful magic, and without which he is a terrified prey to nameless horrors.

This obsessive need to surround oneself with material things, as a substitute for a real sense of security, is not confined to children. It is almost certainly the main reason for the modern disease of acquisitiveness that moralists in both religious and secular Press condemn with much smugness.

The reasons for the lack of a sense of security are not far to seek. Fundamentally it stems from a lack of belief in any kind of God or even any absolute good. But an absence of such belief is

compatible with the persistence of a general
sense of security in a strictly organized society in
which the social hierarchy and the values it em-
bodies are taken for granted by everyone. Such
a state of society does not, of course, rule out
individual suffering and insecurity, but as long
as the structure lasts such cases are interpreted
as exceptions, even by the sufferers. A general
sense of the fundamental rightness of things sup-
ports the fabric of society even when its doctrinal
basis has melted away. When that sense of basic
rightness disintegrates, as it has done in Western
society, insecurity becomes endemic.

It is not hard to see what is wrong and why.
When it comes to putting it right our moralists
falter. Generally, suggested remedies prove to be
no more than exhortations to put the clock back,
sometimes by unspecified means, sometimes by
attempts at escape into small private Utopias
where (again) envy will not exist because there
will be nothing to arouse it.

More often no remedy is suggested. We are
merely told to realize that envy is a sin.

All right—so we root out envy from our souls.
We watch the Joneses drive past in their new
car, and refrain from regretting our five-year-old
model. We are shown the Browns' holiday snaps
from Italy and do not hide the fact that we went
to Bognor. But what happens when a devil is
driven out? We have been warned. The house
left "swept and garnished" is soon inhabited by
a whole family of new and superior devils. We

no longer envy Mrs Smith her new dress or
Mr Smith his promotion. We are above such
paltry desires. We are people of sensibility, un-
worried by material ambitions, unanxious for
the prizes of the status-seekers. For us the simple
life, the distinction of those who value the things
of the mind and spirit. The acceptable devils of
pride have found themselves a comfortable
home.

Is there no way out? Must we jump from the
frying-pan of envy and acquisitiveness into the
fire of pride?

There is another way, and it was experienced
a long time ago by St Francis. The lover of Lady
Poverty did not despise the good things that God
has given us, and though he found his own vocation in the complete abandonment of property
he did not condemn those whose state obliged
them to make use of this world's goods. His vocation and that of his Brothers depended on the
ability of those who had possessions to supply the
needs of the brethren. He never blamed the
possessors of material goods, though he was sorry
for them, because he knew the difficulties and
temptations that beset them, and from which he
had freed himself at one stroke. But the thing
St Francis discovered, and which is available to
even the most wealthy, was a new attitude to
material goods. It was the attitude of enjoyment
without attachment. St Francis himself had this
attitude chiefly to natural things—the sun,
flowers, animals—because his vocation of forcibly

demonstrating the freedom to be found in detachment demanded his abandonment of all but the barest essentials of living. But it is an attitude that is not fundamentally incompatible with the possession of even stupendous wealth, though the occasions when such wealth is justifiable must be comparatively few.

Basically, it means ceasing to regard possessions as really possessed, except in a purely legal and practical way. Personal possession delimits the use of goods in a convenient way. A clear-cut definition of who (be it an individual or a group) has the right to the use of land, equipment, "amenities", premises, and so on, is necessary for the rational functioning of society. Even in a religious community, where personal possessions are renounced, the clothes or tools allocated to each person are intended for the use of that person, and there would be chaos if the sister in the sewing room could never be sure if the scissors she needed would be available because a sister working in the garden might have taken them to cut roses, or the sister-cook thought they would be handy for cutting off bacon rinds.

The concept of private property is necessary for practical living, and for the protection of the right of the individual to his means of livelihood. Because of this there is a tendency to think that there is an absolute distinction between those who renounce personal possession by vow and those who do not. In reality, the religious is simply making explicit, by formal communal rather than individual tenure of goods, the obvious fact that goods of any kind are for use and enjoyment, as and when they are needed. "Possession" in any other sense is nonsense. There is no mystical bond between an inanimate "thing" and a self-conscious human being.

I possess a kitchen table in the sense that I need one when I am cooking, and that if anyone took it away I should be entitled to the protection of the law in any attempt to get it back. But it would be ridiculous to pretend that I possess it in the sense that I have absolute power over it, as God has over his creation. If I smash the thing I shall be considered crazy unless I can produce an excellent reason why this act of destruction was necessary, and could therefore be classed as a "use" of the table, even if a rather odd one. True, I could not be prosecuted for abusing my table, but there would be a right and reasonable feeling that I was behaving badly, because it is tacitly understood, though not often acknowledged, that human beings do not have absolute rights over even inanimate objects. If (to continue a little while with the table) I were to find I no longer needed it, I could sell it or give it away or cut it up and make it into something else, and all of these courses of action would seem normal and reasonable. But if I put it in a shed and let it rot, while no-one would question my legal right to do so, it would certainly be felt that this was a "waste", that it was an *un*reasonable thing to do, even that it was *wrong*, in the sense

5

that I would be depriving someone else, who
might need it, of the use of a perfectly good bit
of furniture.

This quite normal attitude to possessions perhaps goes to show that people do generally understand that possession is relative, not absolute.

The Christian should not need to rely on a
vague feeling to assure him of this. Christians
are expected to ask—and to thank—God for all
the things they need or want. But it is more difficult to take the next step and realize that the
things we want—even need—are not, when we
get them, *ours*, except in the practical or legal
sense mentioned. They are not ours, they are
only for our use. The distinction may be
meaningless in practical terms, but it is all-
important spiritually and psychologically.

Yet it requires a psychological revolution for
an adult to begin to look at his goods as not his
own, but lent for his use and pleasure. In the
adult, with emotional and mental habits fully
formed (including those of compensating for
lack of basic security by acquisitiveness and its
corollary, envy), such a revolution can only be
accomplished by a deliberate and repeated act
of will. But even if it is only occasionally successful, the effect is startling and altogether delightful. It means that things previously regarded as
held by right become, instead, treats. It gets rid
at one stroke of the things that spoil the pleasure
of a new acquisition, whether it be a washing
machine or a new friend. If each thing that

comes is seen as a "bonus", an undeserved personal greeting from God, then it is impossible to envy those who may have more, or to feel ill-used because some other desired good is denied. This attitude does not, of itself, make it possible always to make the right decision when one longs for some new thing and is not sure whether the expense is justified. But it does make a right decision far more likely, because the thing one needs or wants is judged by its value to oneself in usefulness or pleasure, not by whether someone else has a better one.

Although the obsessive desire to acquire things is not easily and completely rooted out, this way of looking at things can help to build up a *real* sense of security, paradoxically based on an honest realization of the contingency of all human pleasures and possessions, and their consequent precariousness. It drives us to search for security in something beyond and above possessions, even the possession of the love of another human being.

This deliberate withdrawal from the sense of possession extends the possibility of enjoyment enormously. If things are enjoyed for themselves and not because they are ours, then it is possible to take pleasure in the roses in a neighbour's garden, the dress in the shop window, the toy that another child is playing with. The pleasure is different, of course. The garden you tended yourself, the dress that "does things for you", the toy that was a special Christmas present, have a

special value. This value is increased if we can
purge ourselves of the fears and envies that go
with feeling that these things are ours by right,
and it does not prevent our enjoyment of beauty,
utility, gaiety, wherever it occurs, whether or not
we are in a position to make the fullest use of its
source. Nobody in their senses resents the fact
that valuable pictures remain in a picture
gallery, and people go, if their tastes lie that way,
to look at them and enjoy them. Yet few women
are able to take pleasure in the beauty of a dress
they cannot afford. Few people can visit the house
of friends and enjoy its comfort and beauty as
such. They will be irritated by the shortcomings
of their own in comparison, or at least a little
saddened at the sight of the unattainable. But
the individual who has fully understood the
gloriously accidental quality of his "own" goods
is free from this sadness or irritation. He is free
to enjoy anything good, anywhere.

We use the word "rights" in unthoughtful
ways. When we talk of the rights of man we can
only mean those things that a man may justly
claim from his fellow men. Correspondingly, it
implies the duty of each to respond to the just
claims of another. But when we talk of our
"rights" we often use the word as if it implied
an absolute right to certain things, as if these
were indispensable to the human condition, so
that we should be in some way invalidated as
human beings if we lacked them. What it often
means is that we feel God "ought" to give us

certain things. God is under no such obligation.
St Francis knew this, all the saints have known
it. Having no sense of their "rights" in relation
to God (though they had a vivid sense of the
"rights" of man in relation to man), they could
take what God gave them with pleasure, and
with a purity of enjoyment usually found only
in children. In renouncing these imaginary
rights in relation to God we are merely acknow-
ledging the actual state of affairs. But it is difficult to do so, difficult to admit our helplessness.
We cling pathetically to our little resentments
because they make us feel we are "somebody", if
only others would recognize the fact. Once we
can manage to face up to our "rightlessness" before God we are free to use and enjoy anything
that comes our way, and much of the sting is removed from "bad luck" and hardships or sorrow.
We know, in theory, that sorrow and suffering in
some measure are the lot of all human beings,
but we still feel there is something wrong when
bad things happen to us. God shouldn't have
done this to *me*. I have a *right* to happiness. We
work ourselves up into a state of resentment
against God (or fate) or look around desperately
for someone to blame, and considerably aggravate the inevitable suffering. But if it is seen as
part of the common lot of humanity, a state of
affairs we do what we can to remedy but from
which we have no right to claim exemption, then
we suffer the unavoidable pain and sorrow, and
no more. It is the reverse side of our pleasure in

the good things that come our way. This attitude
is not the same as the truly supernatural acceptance of suffering as our desirable share in the
redemption of the world by the self-giving of
Christ. The attitude discussed here is a natural
one, within the reach of anyone, but it is the
necessary ground in which more heroic virtues
can grow.

There is one interesting possible by-product
of the release from the itch to possess. Everyone
has to pay taxes of various kinds, open and con-
cealed. Most people acknowledge the necessity
of taxation, though many question the necessity
or wisdom of particular forms of taxation. Christians, like other citizens, have the right and duty
to attempt to effect changes in systems of taxation which they consider wrong. But when it
comes to actually paying taxes we are, after all,
giving money for the benefit of the community
as a whole. We are giving some of what is "ours"
for the use of others. If we did this freely, without
the compulsion of law, it would be considered
generous, patriotic, in every way laudable. But
because we are compelled to pay taxes we feel
there is no room for virtue. Surely, though, freedom is in the will. Paying taxes (local or national)
could be an act of virtue, of justice and even of
charity, if we saw it as a sharing with others of
some part of the goods we receive under the
providence of God. And the compulsory nature
of the payment would then merely deprive us of

the opportunity to spoil this act of sharing by introducing motives of vanity or snobbery.

Highlighting this one aspect of the use of money by a Christian is a reminder that the whole subject of this essay is really money. But thinking of it first of all simply in terms of what money can—or can't—buy is the right way round. It shows that not only money, but also the things money can buy are for use and enjoyment, and have no meaning when regarded as possessions merely. This may seem so obvious that it is hardly worth saying, but the effect of not seeing the obvious is apparent in the ways we think of using money. We think of buying things for our own—or our family's—use as a normal use of money. We think of giving away money, or spending it on others, as exceptional, laudable, but not essential. But if we could once get into the habit of thinking of money as something entrusted to us for our use, we should be more thoughtful about the way we spent it. We should realize that the proper use of money and goods includes their use for the benefit of others, whenever their need outweighs our own need. Primarily our own income and what it buys is for the satisfaction of our own needs—including the need for relaxation and pleasure, in their measure—but a permanent sense of contingency in our hold on material wealth will give a much clearer judgement when it comes to deciding whether another's needs are really greater than our own. It is always a difficult decision, and provided there

is goodwill and a proper sense of values the
objective rightness or wrongness of any particular decision is not of vast importance. Certainly we should not get into a state about it, or
encourage feelings of guilt about those who have
less than we have. As a basic principle it is better
to err on the side of generosity, but there are
so many motives, only a few of which are
normally conscious ones, determining the way
we allocate available "wealth" that it is perhaps
better to be a bit relaxed about it. Once a
decision has been made, right or wrong, it is best
forgotten. If the general attitude is based on a
sure sense of dependence on God for everything,
and in consequence of stewardship, rather than
ownership, of wealth, then the particular
decision will more often be right than wrong,
even judged objectively, and subjectively it will
almost certainly be good.

In the adult the reorientation of ideas about
the possession and use of material wealth can only
be accomplished by a deliberate, and difficult,
act of will, repeated until it becomes a habit,
and inevitably such a transformation of basic
attitudes will be rare. Only a very clear and
enduring conviction of the need for a change can
provide a strong enough motive to begin and
carry through such an undertaking. In the case
of children it is another matter. A child can
learn, from the beginning, to think of material
goods as entrusted to him for his use and
pleasure, which *includes* the use and pleasure of

others when circumstances dictate it. Children grab. "It's mine!" is one of the most frequent cries in the nursery. But all it means is that the child recognizes the goodness of the thing, and wants to be allowed undisputed freedom to enjoy it. This seems a bit of basic good sense. It is right that a human being should want what he perceives to be good. It is only with time and help that a child learns that there is an overriding good that demands that he restrict— voluntarily—his use of any particular good thing. It takes a long time before a child can understand the paramount goodness of things he cannot see or touch. His understanding of the goodness of sharing and giving will develop much more easily if he learns that all the things he uses are given to him *to be used*: for good, his own *and* other people's. It is a reasonable idea to him, even though he finds the practice of it very difficult.

A child who is accustomed to the idea of the contingency of his hold on material things will be much freer to respond to the goodness and beauty of things he does not and cannot "own". People whose minds are set on the feverish desire for the possession of some good thing find it difficult to respond wholeheartedly to anything they cannot possess. They can only think of "good" in terms of "having". This attitude extends, tragically, to people as well as things, and is at the bottom of many unhappy marriages and unstable or unhealthy family relationships.

By helping our children to achieve (so easily, compared with the adult) an habitual sense of dependence, of detachment, of their stewardship of material goods, we are giving them the key to contented and purposeful living.

We are accustomed to the contrast between the attitude of person to thing—I–it—and of person to person—I–thou. But from one point of view this is a false contrast, because it assumes the possibility of a relationship between a person and a thing, and then compares it with that proper between persons. But there is no such thing as a person-to-thing relationship, if the word "relationship" has any real meaning at all. Relationship must be one of person to person; things are used in the development of that relationship, or they can be used to obstruct it. This obstruction happens when things are exalted to the status of persons, and loved, served, desired, as ends, not means. The psychological reasons why this happens are complex; one of them only has been mentioned above. But the fact that it does happen surely helps to show how important it is to have a right attitude to ownership, or rather stewardship, of "possessions". A true sense of stewardship forbids the attribution to things of a value that belongs to persons only. It forbids also the worse, but consequent, aberration of treating persons as if they were things. This may sound contradictory, but it isn't really. Things exalted above their true function are regarded as ends, like persons, but those ends are to subserve the emotional comfort and satisfaction of their owner. Things, thus regarded, are to be slaves, whose function is to serve the lust for power, to pander to the pride of their owner and constantly reassure him of his own value and pre-eminence. They are no longer the vehicles of relationship between human beings, but serve only to exalt one human being in his own eyes and compensate for his basic unease and insecurity. In order that they may do this they must be credited symbolically with attributes no inanimate thing possesses. In the process they lose their true value. But worse still is the devaluation of another human being who is required to subserve the same purpose of the exaltation of the individual, one who is driven to treat them as possessions, over which he has absolute power. The motive is the same in both cases, but of course in the second case the damage is extended to the human victims of this craving for reassurance of value, even of existence.

If this is true then a proper realization of the purpose of "things" is one of the best gifts we can give our children. Not only can this understanding protect them from terrible distortions of human relationships; it can set them free from all kinds of mental and emotional stresses that beset their contemporaries. It can give them the chance to like and be liked, to give and to receive, without reservations. It can open to them enormous opportunities for pleasure and enjoyment that they will otherwise be inhibited from perceiving. If it is worth while for the adult to make the enormous effort required to achieve it, it is even more important to give our children this, their heritage as Christians. For this strange, rare quality of mind is not a new idea. Long before St Francis rediscovered it, it was very simply put: "Blessed are the poor in spirit, the Kingdom of Heaven is theirs."

9

CHARITY BEGINS AT HOME?

T HE essays in this book mostly consider
particular problems of modern Christian
living from the point of view of the individual who has to cope with them. There is a
sense in which this can be a misleading thing to
do, simply because it implies that these problems,
and others, are the responsibility of the individual alone. This implication is too often taken
for granted, yet it should be quite unthinkable
for a Christian.

There are certain facts about modern life in
our kind of society which upset the traditional
pattern we associate with a Christian way of
living. Families can be kept smaller, women can
go out to work, whether from necessity or choice,
the pressure of public opinion that often kept a
marriage from coming unstuck no longer
operates as a clamp in the same way, young
people often have a lot of unsupervised free time
and more money. These are facts, and whether
they are a good or a bad thing is irrelevant.
There they are, and no amount of moaning and
scolding is going to alter them.

Catholics are constantly told that children in
small families miss the formative influence of a

large group to grow up in, that women going out to work produce deprived and possibly delinquent children, that shifting opinion about divorce makes broken marriages more likely, that too much freedom and money encourages both sexual and general irresponsibility in adolescents.

It is undoubtedly true that these situations do frequently produce such effects. But must they necessarily do so? Some would say that the only remedy is to legislate to keep women at home by extra allowances, subsidize large families (regardless of the country's economic position, apparently), tighten up the divorce laws, and exhort parents to keep their adolescents under lock and key. Are we really reduced to this? Quite apart from the fact that it is highly unlikely that such remedies could or would ever be applied, are they even desirable? Or are we making the old mistake of identifying Christianity with the *ancien régime*?

The set of circumstances that I have picked out and which are so often deplored by Christians are not chosen at random. They appear to me, taken together, to offer a challenge and a suggestion of a way of life which would in fact be more, not less, Christian than the old one.

The assumption on which the counsels of despair described above is based is that the old pattern of family living is the only one compatible with Christianity. If we examine it more closely I think we may find that this assumption is quite unwarranted.

The old pattern, which had a lot to be said for it, was based on the single but large family unit, including grandparents, aunts, uncles and so on. Family loyalties were strong, mutual support within the family circle could transcend a lot of personal antipathies or quarrels, blood, as they say, being thicker than water (extra-familial relationships being, presumably, the watery ones). This had its good side, obviously. It was taken for granted that sick or elderly members of the family would have a home and care, though it might sometimes be given grudgingly. Public opinion condemned too strongly the behaviour of neglectful families to make a lonely old age, for instance, a common agony. Children of a large and united family, though they might quarrel, could usually count on each other's support in the last resort. Unwed daughters might be despised but they were not normally thrown out.

But the very strength of loyalties inside the family often made its members indifferent to the needs of those outside. The "tribal" system tended to shrug off all responsibility for people of other "tribes". Those who understood deeply the meaning of Christian brotherhood naturally did not make this mistake, but although the majority accepted that one was obliged to be one's brother's keeper, the definition of a brother remained exceedingly narrow. Still, as a system, it served, while it lasted.

In Western society it has, in the main, ceased to exist. The family unit has shrunk to the basic one of mother, father and children. Grand-parents seldom live with their married children, or vice versa, and when they do it is regarded as an evil, to be escaped when more houses are available. The ambition of every young couple is the privacy of their own home.

The big tight family has become a small tight family, and where this is not the case it is usually only because for some reason a particular section of society has got left behind in the general move-ment of change. But the really important thing about this development is that the little unit is expected to be as self-contained and self-support-ing as the large one was, and it isn't able to be. From this spring unnecessary tensions inside a marriage, gaps in the social and moral formation of the children, loneliness in old age, sexual pro-miscuity among the young who are desperately searching—rightly—for the closeness and warmth of the relationships they lack at home.

So hard-working and dedicated people try to resolve the tensions by marriage counselling, sort out the children in child guidance clinics, run "homes" for the old and provide youth clubs for adolescents. All these things are most neces-sary and the work is invaluable. Only it is surely a little surprising that it seldom occurs to Chris-tians to think that if they lived their faith such things should be only occasionally necessary. I am not saying merely, what we all know, that we should all be more observant of the needs of others, more generous with time and trouble, as *individuals*. It goes much deeper than this. This is a matter of the kind of life that goes on in the local Christian community, *as* a community—the "church" in the Pauline sense. This, and not the family, is the basic Christian unit. It can and should reach out more widely, to other communities, other individuals outside the "church", but it will only do this effectually, as a matter of course, if loyalty and interdependence within the local church are taken for granted just as much as family loyalties are taken for granted when that is the basic unit.

It is worth while to examine the effect of such a sense of unity, not as a means for the spiritual cultivation of the individual Christian but as a practical solution to the sort of problems mentioned at the beginning of this essay, problems that are supposed to be the result of such things as small families, working mothers and comparatively easy divorce. Then perhaps next time we, as Christians, are tempted smugly to condemn the deteriorating morals of modern society we may pause, and wonder, "How much is it *our* fault?"

There are many possible reasons for limiting the number of children in a family, and many means of doing so. I have examined the validity or otherwise of some of the reasons in another

place, and I have no intention of discussing here
the pros and cons of particular methods of family
limitation. Whatever the reasons or the methods,
the fact is that nowadays most couples, Christian
or not, in Western society do limit their families,
and no amount of lecturing and moralizing is
going to stop them. This means that the vast
majority of our children do not grow up in big
families with their discipline of conflicting
moods and wishes, the need for mutual help,
the comfort of mutual support. It seems to be
assumed that this deprivation is inevitable, but
in fact the benefits of having many brothers and
sisters can be obtained equally well when several
smaller families are combined. Sometimes this
happens—and it makes headlines. When a group
of young wives has the sense to pool families and
energies everyone applauds. Why should it be
so unusual? The children benefit enormously.
They have all the fun of games and perhaps
nursery lessons together. They have plenty of
friends, enough people to make proper gangs for
all sorts of games which are impossible in the
smaller family. Yet at the same time they escape
the danger that threatens large families, that the
overworked mother may not be able to give to
each child the individual attention it needs.
There is the big group and the little group, and
the children benefit from both. What is more,
they become much more adaptable than the
single-family child because while they never miss
the security of "my own" Mummy and Daddy

they are accustomed, from an early age, to the care and company of other adults than their parents. The advantage of this in case of the illness of one mother is obvious.

The mothers of the children benefit too. Some women love to be surrounded by small children, but may not be able to manage a large family for financial or health reasons. Some women, devoted to husband, children and home, still long for the "difference" of a part-time job as well. Many mothers would enjoy the chance of further study, or of craft courses, dressmaking or language lessons, and so on. All these needs can be catered for when a group of women work together, and, what is perhaps even more important, the group can arrange to give each mother the chance of a "day off" occasionally, the chance to go out with her husband, perhaps to go on a short holiday with him unencumbered by children. The necessary housework can be got through more quickly without the children, but a daughter, for instance, who needs a cookery lesson need not be interrupted by the needs of younger ones. The children returning to their homes after a day with their little friends, or finding it freshly emptied of lively visitors, value its cosiness and small unity all the more. The mothers, taking their turn, alone or in groups, to look after the children, are undistracted by other cares and can give all their energy and attention to the children. Consequently the children have more constructive fun and quarrel less than when a mother's mind is divided between the needs of the children, the house, and her own desire to sit down and rest. When space is a problem, the chance of finding one room, garage, garden, which is big enough is much greater when several families combine, and trips to the park, or walks in the country, are easier to organize.

Now all this is the sort of thing that any group of women can do; there is nothing especially Christian about it. Or is there? When a child is born to Christian parents he is taken to the local church to be baptized. He is received into the Christian community as a member of Christ. So we are told. But normally the members of the local Christian community, the local "assembly", are absent, apart from the godparents. They are not only absent, they often don't even know the ceremony has taken place and wouldn't feel it was any business of theirs if they did. Yet if the term "body of Christ" means anything, if the word "assembly" is anything more than a description of a crowd, then they both mean that the baby who has just been baptized in our church is our responsibility. We may admit this in theory, but what do we ever do about it?

When a mother is obviously overburdened we are sorry for her. Some people try to help. But it should be a matter of course that the other women of the parish who live near should help, in some such way as suggested above or in others. If it were a normal part of Christian living in the parish those who found it a help would not feel, as they usually do now, that they could not accept help unless they were in a position to do as much in return, or that a mother who let others care for her children was somehow guilty of a dereliction of maternal duty.

Looked at as a part of Christian living the "pooling" of family units could enormously benefit the parish as a whole, forming the basis for larger parish activities. It could release women for training in welfare or Christian Action that would greatly increase their value to the community and also their self-confidence as human beings. This in itself would help to dissipate the discontent that many women feel at being confined to housework and children, and make them more contented, and therefore less self-absorbed, companions for their husbands. It could even happen that husbands and wives might be able to work together over causes that appealed to them both, whether these were amateur dramatics or marriage guidance or whatever.

The young wives' groups which have been so successful are only one way of pooling families. Older women with grown-up children can be an enormous help to younger ones, especially at a stage when the latter are chary of accepting help or advice from their mothers or mothers-in-law and are anxious to prove their ability to cope with things. Real grandparents are an under-rated asset in the family, but when these are not easily accessible "honorary" grandmothers and

grandfathers are invaluable. The artificial isolation of age-groups is a quite unnecessary evil, for
all ages have something to give all the others.
Here again, the sense of mutual dependence and
loyalty in the church should make the help and
pleasure given by old to young and young to old
a normal part of Christian life.

Here the "problems" of small families and
working wives link up with those of frequent
divorce.

Out of the church porch come a young couple
who have just been married. There may be
plenty of guests to drink their health and wish
them well, but probably many of these will have
come some distance. Some may be neighbours
and personal friends, and they are invited as
such. Yet these two are members of the Church,
their mutual vows are not their own responsibility only—their marriage concerns the whole
assembly. The health of this union of Christ and
his Church matters immensely to the health of
the local church itself. One wouldn't think so, to
judge by the general attitude of the normal
parish to its newlyweds. The parish clergy visit
them when they have time, and are always
willing to help if asked. There are plenty of
clubs and groups the couple can join—separately,
as a rule—if they are willing to take the first
step. Or perhaps they are lucky enough to have
Christian neighbours who will make friends with
them. But if this does happen it is exceptional,
certainly not the normal thing. This is not be-

cause most ordinary Christians are mean and selfish and couldn't care less. If they realized a need they would respond, but their formation as Christians has seldom emphasized communal responsibility.

Troubles and tensions in marriage can occur at any time, but they very often happen after the first three or four years, when the novelty has worn off, financial worries are increasing, boredom is pushing its way in. When minor irritations have got out of hand and are assuming critical proportions it is usually too late for an outsider to help, unless one or other of the troubled pair actually seeks advice. Small annoyances become exaggerated in solitary thought. Disagreements or squabbles grow to rows when they are confined between the two people concerned. And when a marriage seems about to break up everyone is sorry or censorious according to temperament, but how often does the local Christian community feel, collectively, "This is *our* fault"?

But if, from the beginning, Christian neighbours assumed that this marriage was their responsibility too, over and over again it would not need to reach the stage where only expert help was of any avail, and even that was perhaps ineffectual. The young wife who felt her husband gave her too little time, help or money could let off steam to a sensible neighbour who would help her to see the thing in proportion and suggest ways of coping. The unappreciated husband, ousted by the baby, could grumble to a trusted friend without embarrassment or a sense of disloyalty, and be helped to see his wife's point of view. Just being able to talk can make all the difference.

From the beginning, the couple should not only be offered help—which can be embarrassing to the young and sensitive—but themselves be asked to help. They could be drawn into the needs of their neighbours, giving hospitality to the lonely, baby-sitting, helping out in a household where there was illness, driving the old and infirm to club, church or hospital, and in all sorts of individual or group work. Being needed by other people, as a unit, could do more to help a couple to grow together and grow up together than many pre-marriage lectures.

This sort of thing does happen, often—but it is always the work of individuals or groups who have unusual insight. It shouldn't be unusual. It should be something that is taught to Christians from the cradle up, for I *am* my brother's keeper. It should be the normal thing that newcomers to the parish should be immediately and deliberately drawn into the life of the parish to the limit of their willingness. It should not be left to them. If their arrival has passed unnoticed by neighbours in a big parish (but it shouldn't, they should be on the lookout) then the clergy should only need to mention their name to nearby families for them to receive a flood of invitations, calls, requests for help. The benefit to the "established" families and individuals would naturally be enormous too.

And if a marriage is in serious difficulties the chances of its being "repaired" with or without professional help are infinitely greater if the couple do not feel themselves to be suffering in isolation but are conscious of the uncensorious concern and sympathy of the "church"—hoping for them, praying for them, expecting the best of them.

The early freedom and earning capacity of the young present tricky problems. Sensible up-bringing makes all the difference, but most adolescents go through a stage when their own parents are not the right people to help them in the difficult adjustment to grown-up life and to their own emotional make-up. They need to break away, to question, even to rebel. Later, if all goes well, they will find their parents again in a new and delightful relationship, but mean-while they need someone else to turn to. Very often a priest only seems like another form of parent, backing up the authority against which they are rebelling.

Mostly they turn to people of their own age. This is a good thing as far as it goes. They need each other and help each other a lot. But adoles-cent ideas and emotions are not yet well related to facts. The new experiences and experiments need some sort of standard against which they can be tested, other than the reaction of those at the same uneasy stage of development. At this time the influence of a family not their own can be of enormous benefit. Other people's parents are seen without the super-critical lens through which teenage children cannot help inspecting their own. Other people's parents can be "mother" and "father" without the complicated emotional relationships from which the young grown-up is trying to break free. If these are good people, who understand their responsibility, such "other" parents can give invaluable help by welcoming the young into their home, listening to confidences when required, giving advice if asked and above all by making them feel that their precarious adulthood is respected and their problems accepted as real.

This happy relationship cannot usually begin when the need for it begins, but it will occur quite naturally where families have lived together, worked and played together, swapped mothers and fathers, borrowed each other's clothes and homes, shared parties or holidays, nursed each other's illnesses, cleaned each other's houses, celebrated each other's feasts and mourned each other's sorrows from their earliest years. Youth clubs are excellent, so are many other organizations for the young, but nothing can replace the natural mixture of ages and sexes and interests and talents and needs that can occur quite naturally in a "family", and more especially when this "family" is not confined to the narrow group of blood-relations but extends in ever-growing units through groups of families, the parish, and beyond.

Into this community older and single people fit without difficulty, and here again most people prefer to be needed than to be helped. Those whose help has been asked as baby-sitters, handymen, emergency nurses, honorary grandparents, occasional "home helps" will be far more able to accept happily and without humiliation the help that is offered them in the time of their own need.

At the risk of being unjust to many farsighted and enlightened clergy, it is worth asking what appears to be the order of priority given to aspects of Christian living as presented from Catholic pulpits. The list goes something like this: Sunday Mass comes a safe first, followed by chastity; sending the children to Catholic schools; money for the schools; family prayers; devotion to Mary; the need to encourage priestly vocations; money for the missions; penance; avoiding "bad" books, films, TV shows; setting a good example to non-Catholics. Somewhere way down the list comes something about praying for the Council, and perhaps a mention of the need for mutual charity. (Oh yes—I nearly forgot—the need for "good old-fashioned discipline" at home comes fairly high on the list.)

All these things may be important, some are enormously important, but there does seem to be a basic confusion of means and ends. Even the Mass is not an end in itself but a means towards living more fully the Christ-life to which our baptism dedicates us. The confusion is not necessary. Sketched here are just a few of the benefits that could result from looking at the conditions of modern life not as an enemy to be condemned and fought but as a marvellous opportunity for a more fully Christian way of living. Whether these facts of modern life become our enemies or our allies as Christians depends entirely on the kind of ideal of Christian living that is presented to ordinary Christians.

We have largely lost the sense of community, yet this is what Christianity, as a way of life, is about. The love of one's neighbour is not an optional extra for saints but the essential condition not only of personal salvation—as Christ pointed out frequently and with considerable force—but for the very existence of the Church as the body of Christ. The Church—and the local church—is the new Israel. Hear, O Israel. The Lord your God, the Lord is one. And you must love the Lord your God with all your heart and soul and strength. This is the first commandment—but the second is like it. You must love your neighbour as yourself. Who is my neighbour? We know the answer to that one.

You might also be interested in

Edited by

Yves Congar, O.P., Hans Kung,
Daniel O'Hanlon, S.J.

COUNCIL SPEECHES OF VATICAN II

6/- net

"These speeches are the record of a dazzling renewal and the symbol of immeasurable hope, so dynamic, indeed, as to be disconcerting to those whose Catholicism is much involved—understandably—with the comfort of familiar habit. But need even the most conservative really be afraid? The Apostles were doubtless somewhat disconcerted at Pentecost; yet the fire of the Holy Spirit does not destroy; it renews the face of the earth."

Ducketts Register

If you wish to order this book cut this out and hand it to your local bookseller or in case of difficulty send direct to Sheed & Ward, Ltd., 33 Maiden Lane, London, W.C.2

Please send me........copy/ies

Name..

Address...

....

....

Payment on receipt of invoice